D1477255

.

IPSWICH TOWN
Miscellany

IPSWICH TOWN
Miscellany

Blues Trivia,
History, Facts & Stats

DAN BOTTEN

IPSWICH TOWN
Miscellany

All statistics, facts and figures are correct as of 1st August 2015

© Dan Botten

Dan Botten has asserted his rights in accordance with the Copyright, Designs and Patents Act 1988 to be identified as the author of this work.

Published By:
Pitch Publishing (Brighton) Ltd
A2 Yeoman Gate
Yeoman Way
Durrington
BN13 3QZ

Email: info@pitchpublishing.co.uk
Web: www.pitchpublishing.co.uk

First published 2009
Reprinted 2015

A catalogue record for this book is available from the British Library.

10-digit ISBN: 1-9054115-4-5
13-digit ISBN: 978-1-9054115-4-2

Printed and bound in Great Britain by TJ International

This book is dedicated to all my family

for their love, support and patience.

Special thanks to Hilary, Alex and the bump

who continue to make everything worthwhile.

FOREWORD BY MATT HOLLAND

I am extremely honoured to have been given the privilege of writing the foreword to this book. So many great players have represented the club with distinction and I am thrilled to have played a small part in the club's rich history.

Ipswich Town Football Club is special – very special – and from the moment I signed to the day I die nothing will change my mind to the contrary. I have so many happy and special memories from my time at the club it is impossible to pass them all on to you in this short passage, but I will give it a go!

My journey at the club began in 1997, signing from AFC Bournemouth. I remember negotiations over my signature taking ages. I was very frustrated because I just wanted the opportunity to play at a higher level. Although not a supporter in my younger days, Ipswich was a team I had a lot of admiration for after watching the likes of John Wark, Paul Mariner, the Dutch maestros Muhren and Thijssen – to name just a few – not forgetting a man who would soon be my manager, George Burley. On my arrival I wasn't disappointed. A fantastic stadium and training facilities, good players, loyal and wonderful fans with whom I would strike up an immediate rapport, and perhaps most importantly, from the chairman down to the kit man, very good people.

My six years at the club contained the inevitable highs and lows but fortunately the good times outweighed the bad. My most abiding memory would probably be the play-off win at Wembley against Barnsley. After three consecutive semi-final defeats we would eventually gain promotion to the Premier League with a thrilling 4-2 victory. I will never forget the noise from the sea of blue and white fans and the pride I had in lifting a trophy in their direction. I will always remember the bus journey back to Ipswich by the volume of people on the bridges of the A12 and also by the number of times we sang Oasis' Wonderwall!!

Other great memories include finishing fifth in the Premier League – only being denied a Champions League place on the final day of the season by Liverpool, and who could forget beating Inter Milan in the Uefa Cup at Portman Road. Winning the supporters' Player of the Year in my first season is another obvious highlight – to do it again in my last season and join an elite band of just four players to have won it twice (Kevin Beattie, John Wark and Terry Butcher the others) was extra special.

I signed off with Ipswich at Derby County – scoring with my last kick for the club in a 4-1 win. Although not wanting to leave, it was I suppose the perfect way to go. I can quite honestly say I loved every minute of my time at the club. So much so that I still live in the area and try to get to Portman Road as often as I can. Although not a supporter as a child, I certainly am now.

The club is entering a new era under the leadership of Roy Keane and I am convinced that good times lie around the corner. In the meantime I hope you enjoy the book and that it provokes some of your own wonderful memories.

Matt Holland made 259 appearances for Ipswich and scored 38 goals over the course of six years. He was Supporters' Player of the Year twice and played and scored for the Republic of Ireland at the 2002 World Cup Finals.

INTRODUCTION

Ipswich Town is a football club held in high esteem by many outside the Suffolk boundaries in which it resides. The vast majority of football fans, when asked to recall a trip to Portman Road or their memories of the club, generally allude to a friendly place to visit, a team who try and play good football and then name a procession of players who would grace the teamsheets of every club in the country.

Indeed it seems that almost every black cab driver in London I have ended up talking to can reel off either half of the 1981 Uefa Cup-winning team or that the bloke who scored the winning goal in the FA Cup final victory in 1970-something promptly collapsed and was substituted!

However, when researching and compiling this book, it amazed me that it is not just the obvious or memorable that has positioned this club near the top of the English footballing tree. Many gems have been unearthed from hours of research across a range of club publications and internet sites, most notably www.tmwmtt.com and the magnificent *The Men Who Made The Town.*

Finally, of course, thanks to the all the players, staff and management who have helped to shape the history of Ipswich Town Football Club and whose stories sit at the heart of a never-ending tale of joy, sorrow, defeat and victory.

Dan Botten, August 2009

CORINTHIAN SPIRIT PREVAILS

At a special meeting of Ipswich Town Football Club in April 1895, the chance to move into professional football was turned down due to costs and the fact that football was to be "played for fun and not become a business". R. D. Hendry, a local businessman, was the lone voice to propose Town employ a professional team but was not successful.

INAUGURAL HALL OF FAMERS

Before the Blues drubbed Sheffield Wednesday 4-1 on the opening game of the season at Portman Road in 2007, the newly created Ipswich Town Hall of Fame welcomed its first four inductees. What legends they were! Ray Crawford – Town's top goalscorer of all time with 227 goals in 353 appearances – was first. He was followed by strike partner Ted Phillips. Phillips scored 46 goals when Town won the championship in 1956/1957 – the highest goalscorer in a single season for the club. Glaswegian John Wark, Town's top-scoring midfielder and proud owner of 678 appearances in three Suffolk spells was followed by Mick Mills, who sits top of the Portman Road appearance charts with 741 appearances. Between them, these four players had scored 615 goals – including 21 hat-tricks – made over 2,000 Blues outings, won ten medals and represented their countries on 73 occasions.

MAN UNITED MAULED

On a famous Saturday in March 1980, gangly striker Paul Mariner scored a hat-trick as Town walloped second-placed Manchester United 6-0 at Portman Road. United keeper Gary Bailey, son of Portman Road legend Roy, was his team's hero, saving three penalties on a dramatic afternoon in Suffolk.

THE THIEF OF BAGHDAD

In March 1986, Bobby Ferguson took his troops away from the cold winter weather, and on a questionable 15-hour trip to Baghdad to play an Iraq National XI. Trevor Putney's strike won the game for Town in front of just 3,000 fans.

WE'VE GOT A NORTHERN IRISH INTERNATIONAL...

Pat Sharkey

Position	Midfielder
Born	Omagh, August 26th 1953
Town Hello	(A) Manchester City, 25/10/75, D1, D 1-1
Town Farewell	(H) Middlesbrough, 23/4/77, D1, L 0-1
Town/Intl Appearances	19/1
Town/Intl Goals	1/0

One of just a handful of Omagh-born players to play at the highest level, Sharkey joined Ipswich in September 1973 but had to wait over two years for his league debut. He played 18 league games, scoring just once in a 2-1 win at Arsenal in April 1976. He was awarded his only cap against Scotland in May 1976. It was a disappointing match all round – Scotland, 2-0 up at half-time, cruised to an easy 3-0 win with Sharkey replaced after 61 minutes.

WE'VE GOT A SCOTTISH INTERNATIONAL...

Alan Brazil

Position	Striker
Born	Glasgow, June 15th 1959
Town Hello	(H) Manchester United, 14/1/78, D1, L 1-2
Town Farewell	(A) WBA, 12/3/83, D1, L 1-4
Town/Intl Appearances	210/11
Town/Intl Goals	80/0

The ebullient Brazil won eleven full Scottish caps whilst an Ipswich player and two more after his transfer to Tottenham Hotspur for £470,000 in March 1983. He also gained eight under-21 caps and represented his country at youth level. Town snapped up Brazil under the gaze of Celtic in 1977 and he turned into a consistent goalscorer at the club – his best season being 1981-1982 when he finished top of the charts with 28 goals in 44 games. Since hanging up his boots, Brazil has enjoyed a successful media career, and hosts Talksport's breakfast show.

BRAZIL NUT: SCOTTISH STRIKER ALAN BRAZIL SCORED 80 BLUES GOALS

WE'RE ALL GOING ON A EUROPEAN TOUR

At the end of the 1910-11 season Ipswich – then competing in the Southern Amateur League – made their first visit to the Continent at the invitation of Czech side SK Slavia. Departing on Wednesday 3rd May they travelled by boat and train across Holland, Belgium, Germany and Czechoslovakia to Prague, arriving on the Friday. They played two matches against SK Slavia that weekend, losing the first game 4-0 and drawing the second 1-1. William 'Billy' F. Garnham, club captain at the time, was in charge of the tour party, which included several guest players from Bury United, and numbered fifteen in all. Today, SK Slavia play at the 21,000 capacity Eden Stadium, but at the time of Town's visit 'The Sewns' played at the Letna Stadium – their home from the 1890s until 1953 – and the two games against Ipswich drew respectable crowds of 3,000 and 4,500. The Czechs were coached by former Scotland player John Madden. Madden presided over team matters from 1905 to 1930 – a highly successful era for the club – during which they won the Czechoslovak title four times, the Bohemian title twice, the CSF title twice and the Bohemia Cup on five occasions.

TOWN GAFFERS

The most successful managers of Ipswich Town based on percentage of league and cup games won – excluding caretaker managers and since the club entered The Football League in 1938 – are:

	P	W	%
Sir Alf Ramsey	369	176	48%
George Burley	413	188	46%
Sir Bobby Robson	709	316	45%
John Duncan	161	73	45%
Joe Royle	189	81	43%
Scott Duncan	505	205	41%
Bill McGarry	196	80	41%
Mick McCarthy	134	55	41%
Jim Magilton	148	56	38%
Bobby Ferguson	258	97	38%
Roy Keane	81	28	35%
Paul Jewell	85	29	34%

PORTMAN ROAD LEGENDS

Doug Rees

Position	Centre-half
Born	Neath, February 12th 1923
Town Hello	(A) Leyton Orient, 9/4/49, D3 (S), D 1-1
Town Farewell	(H) Grimsby Town, 11/4/59, D2, W 2-1
Appearances	386
Goals	1

Doug 'Dai' Rees was already a Welsh international amateur centre-half when he joined The Town from Troedyhriw in 1949. The Blues made a donation of £350 to the Welsh club and it proved to be money well spent as over exactly ten years' magnificent service Rees helped the club to win the Division Three (South) title in the 1953/1954 season. The popular defender only scored one goal in his Town career which came in a 2-2 draw at Shrewsbury Town in 1952/1953 after he was pressed into emergency service as a centre-forward. Like John Elsworthy, Rees narrowly missed out on a place in the Welsh squad for the 1958 World Cup Finals and after leaving the club enjoyed spells at local non-league clubs before working at William Brown's timber merchants for many years.

THE FRANK & ALLAN SHOW

A thrilling 2-2 Division One draw at Leeds United in 1972 was a day for the Clarke family to remember. England striker Allan Clarke scored the equaliser for the hosts after his elder brother Frank had opened the scoring for the Blues. Frank Clarke scored 17 goals for Ipswich over four seasons after signing from Queens Park Rangers for £40,000. He was the only one of the footballing Clarke siblings not to play for Walsall – Allan, Derek and Wayne all played for the Midlands side.

WARK'S WOE

In March 1995, John Wark became the first ever Blues player to be sent off against Norwich City in a 3-0 Premier League defeat at Carrow Road minutes before the break. In another notable first, it was George Burley's first game against City as Town manager.

COBBOLD CALAMITIES

Captain John 'Ivan' Murray Cobbold was Town chairman from 1936 to 1944. A former Eton schoolboy and Scots Guard, 'Ivan' became president of the old amateur club in June 1935, having served in a similar role at the Suffolk County FA during the preceding two years. He first became chairman of the newly formed Ipswich Town Football Club Ltd as the club embraced professionalism in May 1936. As a result of his drive and determination – just two years after turning professional – Town were elected to the Football League in 1938. Sadly, having witnessed just one season of league football at Portman Road, before the outbreak of WWII, he was killed by a German flying bomb whilst attending a private service at The Royal Guards Chapel in London in June 1944. His second son, Patrick, joined the board in June 1964 and became the fifth Cobbold family member to become chairman when he was appointed in 1976. During his reign he enjoyed Town's 1978 FA Cup and 1981 Uefa Cup victories. Incredibly, he narrowly avoided serious injury, even death, when he was in the foyer of the London Hilton ten minutes before it was bombed by the IRA in September 1975 when two people were killed and 63 injured. The next day he watched Town draw 0-0 at Coventry City.

PLAY-OFF PARTICULARS

Town's play-off record and goalscorers – 1987 to 2005:

Played..17
Won..4
Drawn 6
Lost 7
Scored...24
Conceded..28

Goalscorers : Jim Magilton (3), Marcus Stewart (3), Kieron Dyer (2), Martijn Reuser (2), Matt Holland (2), Darren Bent (1), James Scowcroft (1), Jamie Clapham (1), Mick Stockwell (1), Niklas Gudmundsson (1), Richard Naylor (1), Shefki Kuqi (1), Steve McCall (1), Tony Mowbray (1), Tommy Smith (1), Paul Anderson (1), og (1).

WE'VE GOT A BULGARIAN INTERNATIONAL...

Bontcho Guentchev

Position ....Striker
Born .... Bulgaria, July 7th 1964
Town Hello .... (H) Manchester City, 12/12/92, PL, W 3-1
Town Farewell............................... (A) Leeds United, 5/4/95, PL, L 0-4
Town/Intl Appearances 75/7
Town/Intl Goals... 11/0

Signed from Sporting Lisbon in 1992 alongside Vlado Bozinowski, who acted at his interpreter, Bulgarian Guentchev burst on to the Portman Road scene with a marvellous hat-trick against Grimsby Town in the FA Cup. Although lightweight, Guentchev possessed excellent technical ability which he displayed as his country reached the 1994 World Cup finals thanks to Guentchev scoring a vital penalty in the second round shoot-out against Mexico. After leaving Ipswich he joined Luton Town before running a bar called 'Strikers' in West London which now has sadly closed.

HOME SWEET HOME

In April 1981, goals from Charlie Nicholas and Kenny Sansom led Arsenal to a 2-0 victory at Portman Road in Division One and ended an incredible run of 46 Portman Road games undefeated for Town.

DEFENSIVE DISASTERS

In a woeful 1963-64 season, which saw the Town relegated and manager Jackie Milburn dismissed, the Blues went down 9-1 at Stoke City in Division One. Dennis Viollet, who survived the Munich air disaster, scored a hat-trick which was a fortnight after Ipswich were crushed 6-0 at Liverpool.

THE FIRST POT OF MANY

In 1887, Ipswich landed their first ever trophy when Ipswich Association beat Ipswich School 2-1 in the Suffolk Challenge Cup Final at Portman Road. In snowy conditions, Sherrington and Peecock scored the goals in front of 1,000 spectators.

FROM CARDIFF TO WEMBLEY

Ipswich began their 1978 FA Cup-winning campaign with a comfortable 2-0 victory against Cardiff City at Ninian Park. Mick Mills marked a club appearance record at the time of 494 Town games with an excellent display while Paul Mariner struck both goals in front of 13,584 fans – Ninian Park's biggest gate of the season.

PORTMAN ROAD LEGENDS

Mick Mills

Position .... Full-back
Born .... Godalming, January 4th 1949
Town Hello .... (H) Wolverhampton W, 7/5/66, D2, W 5-2
Town Farewell .... (A) Liverpool, 26/10/82, LC, L 0-2
Appearances 741
Goals 30

Signed from Portsmouth in February 1966, Mills won 42 caps for England during his 16 years at Portman Road before leaving for Southampton in November 1982 after captaining his country at the World Cup finals in Spain the previous summer. As Town skipper he lifted the FA Cup in 1978 and the Uefa Cup in 1981. Ever present in four successive seasons from 1972/1973, appearing in 198 consecutive league games, Mick Mills was also capped by England at youth and under-23 levels, and represented the Football League before managing Stoke City and Colchester United.

CREWE DERAILED

Under manager Joe Royle, Town inherited a Jekyll and Hyde personality which saw them score goals by the bucketload but concede in almost equal measures. Against Crewe Alexandra at Portman Road in January 2004, the Railwaymen were pipped 6-4 in a titanic battle. Midfielder Tommy Miller and Finn Shefki Kuqi scored twice while half of Crewe's tally came from own goals by Matt Richards and John McGreal. Spaniard Pablo Counago and flying Dutchman Martijn Reuser goals sealed a breathless affair.

SUPER MICK: FULL-BACK MICK MILLS KEEPS HIS EYE ON THE BALL

FORTRESS PORTMAN ROAD

Town's biggest home victories since turning professional in 1936
(by 7 goals or more):

31/10/1936	Cromer	11-0	FA Cup
25/9/1962	Floriana	10-0	European Cup
3/10/1936	Stowmarket Town	8-0	FA Cup
19/9/1936	Eastern Counties United	7-0	FA Cup
30/4/1938	Aldershot Reserves	7-0	Southern League
26/11/1938	Street	7-0	FA Cup
7/11/1964	Portsmouth	7-0	Division Two
2/2/1974	Southampton	7-0	Division One
6/11/1976	West Brom	7-0	Division One
3/10/1979	Skied Oslo	7-0	Uefa Cup
29/8/2002	Avenir Beggen	8-1	Uefa Cup

PORTMAN ROAD LEGENDS

John Wark

Position	Midfield
Born	Glasgow, August 4th 1949
Town Hello	(N) Leeds United, 27/3/75, FAC, W 3-2
Town Farewell	(A) Tranmere Rovers, 30/11/96, D1, L 0-3
Appearances	678
Goals	179

One of the finest players to have graced the Portman Road turf, Wark bestrode opposition midfields throughout the 1970s and 1980s as a colossus. He scored 14 goals in 12 games from midfield during the 1981 Uefa Cup and was awarded PFA Player of the Year at the end of the season – he also won the European Young Footballer of the Year that term. Wark collected 29 caps for Scotland and scored seven international goals as well as enjoying spells at Liverpool and Middlesbrough. A magnificent servant who enjoyed three spells at Portman Road, John acted as joint caretaker-manager with Paul Goddard before George Burley was appointed.

THE MEN WHO MANAGED THE TOWN I

Mick O'Brien
Spell: May 1936 to August 1937
Honours: Southern League Champions 1936/1937
Overall record: P 39; W 25 D 9 L 5 F 107 A 42

O'Brien became Town's first manager as a professional club in May, 1936. He had previously been assistant manager at Brentford and managed Queens Park Rangers. An Irish-born strapping centre-half he served in both the Royal Navy and Royal Flying Corps during World War I. The death of his wife and resulting personal problems led to his departure just over 14 months later from Portman Road after bringing the club the Southern League title (the club's first professional honour).

LIVE FROM PORTMAN ROAD

The *Match of the Day* cameras were at Portman Road for the first ever 'live' transmission of a home game in January 1988 as Town crashed to a 2-1 defeat to Manchester United in the FA Cup third round. Stalwart defender Tony Humes scored with a crunching header as United were held at the break before England international Viv Anderson scored the winner for the visitors late on.

TEN'S UP

There have been seven instances of Town games which have seen ten goals scored or more since turning professional. Two of these were trouncings at Fulham and Stoke City which came within three months in the grim 1963/1964 season under Jackie Milburn.

11	31/10/1936	Cromer (H)	FAC	11-0
11	9/9/1948	Notts County (A)	D3(S)	2-9
11	26/12/1963	Fulham (A)	D1	1-10
10	16/10/1937	Newport County Reserves (H)	SL	8-2
10	25/9/1962	Floriana (H)	EC	10-0
10	21/3/1964	Stoke City (A)	D1	1-9
10	17/1/2004	Crewe Alexandra (H)	D1	6-4

SUPPORTERS' PLAYER OF THE SEASON

Kevin Beattie 1972-73
Kevin Beattie 1973-74
Colin Viljoen 1974-75
Allan Hunter 1975-76
George Burley.......................................1976-77
Mick Mills 1977-78
Arnold Muhren 1978-79
Frans Thijssen 1979-80
Paul Cooper 1980-81
Alan Brazil.......................................1981-82
Paul Mariner.......................................1982-83
Trevor Putney 1983-84
Terry Butcher.......................................1984-85
Terry Butcher.......................................1985-86
Romeo Zondervan 1986-87
Frank Yallop.......................................1987-88
John Wark.......................................1988-89
John Wark.......................................1989-90
David Linighan 1990-91
John Wark.......................................1991-92
Mick Stockwell.......................................1992-93
John Wark.......................................1993-94
Craig Forrest.......................................1994-95
Simon Milton 1995-96
Mauricio Taricco.......................................1996-97
Matt Holland.......................................1997-98
Jamie Clapham 1998-99
Jamie Scowcroft.......................................1999-2000
Marcus Stewart.......................................2000-01
Mark Venus.......................................2001-02
Matt Holland.......................................2002-03
Ian Westlake 2003-04
Shefki Kuqi.......................................2004-05
Fabian Wilnis 2005-06
Sylvain Legwinski 2006-07
Jon Walters.......................................2007-08

Richard Wright.....................................2008-09
Gareth McAuley 2009/2010
Jimmy Bullard..................................2010/2011
Aaron Creswell 2011/2012
Tommy Smith 2012/2013
Christophe Berra 2013/2014
Daryl Murphy..................................2014/2015

PORTMAN ROAD LEGENDS

Eric Gates

Position	Forward
Born	Ferryhill, June 28th 1955
Town Hello	(H) Wolves, 27/10/73, D1, W 2-0
Town Farewell	(H) West Ham, 17/5/85, D1, L 0-1
Appearances	384
Goals	96

One of many players to graduate from the youth team, the diminutive striker made his Town debut in 1973 but would have to wait until the 1977/78 season, though, before he became a regular face in the first-team line-up. Gates won two full caps, under then England manager Ron Greenwood, during the 1980/81 season and played in all but one of the Town's Uefa Cup-winning games, collecting a winners' medal in Amsterdam. He also scored a vital away goal for Town against Aris Salonika of Greece. His final appearance in a Town shirt was alongside Russell Osman against West Ham in May 1985. After spells at Sunderland and Carlisle United, Gates found his way into the world of broadcasting and now works for Century FM.

ICE ICE MAYBE

Town's 0-0 FA Cup fourth round tie with Leyton Orient went ahead after flamethrowers cleared ice from the Churchmans' End goalmouth. With more than 40 league and cup matches were postponed that day in January 1979 due to Arctic conditions, Ipswich were keen to play as they were in form and on a five game unbeaten run. A brace from Paul Mariner won the replay at Brisbane Road for the FA Cup holders three days later.

WE'VE GOT A CANADIAN INTERNATIONAL...

Craig Forrest

Position	Goalkeeper
Born	Vancouver, September 20th 1967
Town Hello	(A) Stoke City, 27/8/88, D2, D 1-1
Town Farewell	(H) Oxford United, 22/2/97, D1, W 2-1
Town/Intl Appearances	312/42
Town/Intl Goals	0/0

Gangling Craig Forrest earned 57 caps in the Canadian goalkeeper jersey, 42 of them while at Portman Road. He starred in Canada's World Cup qualifying campaign for USA 1994, in which his side narrowly missed out on a play-off decider with Argentina for a place in the finals, drawing over two legs with Australia but going out on a penalty shoot-out. Forrest arrived in the UK after paying his own air fare, so confident was he that he would earn a professional contract. An excellent shot-stopper, Forrest became a firm favourite with the Suffolk faithful.

A NEW DEFINITION OF ROW Z

On Saturday 17th November 1894, in a 1-0 win at Colchester Town, Ipswich's Stanley Turner's shot cleared the stand and landed on a horse ploughing a nearby field. The horse bolted and ploughed the fastest, if not the straightest, furrow on record.

OSBORNE'S AMAZING FIVE MONTHS

When Ipswich travelled to Highbury to take on Arsenal on Monday January 2nd 1978, little did they know that the two teams would meet at Wembley only five months later in the FA Cup final. Town's miserable away record that season continued with a shot-shy 1-0 defeat against The Gunners in front of 43,705 fans. Roger Osborne came on as a second-half substitute to little impact. Osborne's fortunes would change significantly on that balmy day at Wembley when he would have to be replaced due to exhaustion after scoring the winning goal to earn Town a famous triumph.

TOP 10 PORTMAN ROAD ATTENDANCES

38,010 vs Leeds United ......(FA Cup sixth round) 1974-75
35,109 vs Liverpool.............(Division One) 1976-77
35,077 vs Norwich City......(Division One) 1975-76
34,726 vs Norwich City......(Division One) 1976-77
34,709 vs Liverpool.............(FA Cup fourth round).................1974-75
34,636 vs Arsenal ....(Division One) 1972-73
33,663 vs Barcelona.............(Uefa Cup third round, first leg)...1977-78
33,438 vs Manchester U .....(Division One) 1975-76
33,292 vs Liverpool.............(Division One) 1973-74
32,996 vs Wolves.................(FA Cup fourth round).................1976-77

THE GOAL THAT NEVER WAS

In the 1970/71 campaign – Bobby Robson's second full season in charge at Portman Road – Town were involved in perhaps the most controversial incident of the season when, in a league encounter with Chelsea at Stamford Bridge, Alan Hudson scored the "goal that never was". The Londoners' midfielder sent in a shot that went into the side netting, to the right of Town keeper David Best, hitting the rear stanchion and rebounding back onto the pitch. As Best collected the ball in readiness to take the goal kick, referee Roy Capey amazed everyone by awarding the home side a goal. Following protestations by the Ipswich players he conferred with the linesman but stuck with his original decision. Capey and his assistant were obviously the only two people in the ground who held that opinion and were proven wrong by photographic evidence that was made available later. Chelsea went on to win the game 2-1, and Bobby Robson's call to the Football League to have the game replayed was turned down.

MOODY YOUDS

On September 26th 1992, Canadian keeper Craig Forrest received his marching orders after only two minutes of the home game against Sheffield United. His Scouse team-mate Eddie Youds, in particular, would not have been happy. He was hauled off and replaced by Clive Baker who expertly went on to keep a clean sheet in a goalless draw.

HERO TO VILLAIN

Adam Tanner, a tall midfielder born in Essex, was to have a chequered Town career. He scored on his debut against Leicester City in the Premier League in 1995 – his superb volley won the Goal of the Season award from the Portman Road faithful – and not long after scored the winning goal at Anfield as Town won at Liverpool for the first ever time. However, in 1997, he received a three-month ban from the FA when testing positive for cocaine and was banned for three months. Then, in November 1999, Tanner was arrested after the Mercedes-Benz he was driving collided with a parked Vauxhall Cavalier in Witham. Although he failed to stop at the scene of the accident he was later arrested and a blood test showed that he was three times over the legal alcohol limit for driving. In January 2000 he admitted the offence in court and it later emerged that it was his second drink-driving offence in ten years, but in February 2000 he was spared a prison sentence and instead ordered to do 80 hours of community service, placed on probation for 12 months and banned from driving for three years. He was released by Ipswich the same month and made sporadic appearances for Colchester United before moving into non-league football.

WE'VE GOT A CANADIAN INTERNATIONAL...

Jaime Peters

Position	Midfielder
Born	Ontario, May 4th 1987
Town Hello	(H) Cardiff City, 6/8/05, FLC, W 1-0
Town Farewell	Current player
Town/Intl Appearances	48/5
Town/Intl Goals	2/1

Speedy Peters turned down offers to join Manchester United and Chelsea and several other leading clubs after impressing on trial to join Town in the summer of 2005. He was recommended to the club by former favourite Frank Yallop and, although never a regular at the club to date, impressed in the first few games of the Roy Keane era. Peters has earned five caps for Canada whilst at Portman Road which included a 3-2 defeat to Brazil and has scored against Panama.

FA CUP FINAL 1978

Saturday May 6th

Ipswich Town	1-0 (0-0)	Arsenal
Osborne 77		Att 100,000

1. Paul Cooper	1. Pat Jennings
2. George Burley	2. Pat Rice
3. Mick Mills (captain)	3. Sammy Nelson
4. Brian Talbot	4. David Price
5. Allan Hunter	5. David O'Leary
6. Kevin Beattie	6. Willie Young
7. Roger Osborne (Mick Lambert)	7. Liam Brady (Graham Rix)
8. John Wark	8. Alan Sunderland
9. Paul Mariner	9. Malcolm Macdonald
10. David Geddis	10. Frank Stapleton
11. Clive Woods	11. Alan Hudson

At long last Town won a major trophy which their steady progress under Bobby Robson had merited since he was appointed manager nearly ten years previously. Against all the odds, a patched up and unfancied Ipswich won the FA Cup for the first time in their history – on their Wembley debut – with a late goal by Roger Osborne, a local lad and one of many Blue heroes on an unforgettable afternoon at Wembley. Town had dominated the game so conclusively, that until Osborne scored there was a feeling that whoever, or whatever it is, that frowns upon Ipswich's endeavours would force them to remain empty-handed once more. Paul Mariner hit the bar in the first half and John Wark twice thudded Jenning's posts with fierce shots as The Blues swarmed all over a beleaguered Gunners side in the second half. Arsenal, hot favourites, were totally outplayed despite, on paper, having a superior line-up, and were shaken right from the off as David Geddis – playing only because Trevor Whymark was not fully fit after a knee injury – turned in a superb performance. Playing on the right-hand side, Geddis caused panic in the Arsenal ranks with his direct runs and it was he that made the opening for the goal that forever transformed Town into something considerably livelier than a sleepy East Anglian town for days to come. A sudden break by Geddis down the right – who flew past Hudson and Nelson – saw him drive the ball low into the area which Willie Young could only block to Osborne who crashed the ball back into the net. Exhaustion and overwhelming emotion followed which meant he had to be replaced by Mick Lambert and just over ten minutes later Suffolk began the rejoicing to which they were fully entitled.

THE MEN WHO MANAGED THE TOWN

Sir Alf Ramsey
Spell: August 1955 to April 1963
Honours: Division Three (South) Champions 1956/57,
Division Two Champions 1960/61,
Division One Champions 1961/62
Overall Record: P 369 W 176 D 75 L 118 F 723 A 584

Born in Dagenham, Essex, in 1920, Alf Ramsey played for Southampton and Tottenham Hotspur as an elegant defender, winning two league titles at White Hart Lane and 32 caps for his country. After retiring from Spurs, he was appointed manager of Town and led the club to an amazing era of success including the Third Division (South) title in 1956/1957, the Second Division championship in 1960/1961 and the First Division championship in 1961/1962. This was one of the most remarkable top-flight wins in history as the press and many pundits had consigned the club to almost certain relegation. His tactical astuteness was legendary and he got the very maximum out of a squad of hard-working, solid players and it was not surprising when England came calling and appointed him manager in January 1963. He gave the country its greatest footballing triumph – winning the World Cup in 1966 – using some of the tactics that had led Town to so much success by ditching orthodox wingers in favour of attacking midfielders who could both defend as well as running at centre-backs instead of full-backs. This system was known as the 'Wingless Wonders'. After losing only 17 of 113 games for England he was sacked and joined Birmingham City as manager in 1977. Sir Alf Ramsey Way, formerly Portman Walk, was named after Ramsey shortly after his death in 1999 in honour of his achievements as Town manager. In 2000, a statue of Ramsey was erected on the corner of the street named after him and Portman Road. The statue was commissioned by the Ipswich Town Supporters' Club after an initial idea by local fan Seán Salter.

PORTMAN ROAD LEGENDS

George Burley

Position .... Right-back
Born .... Cumnock, June 3rd 1956
Town Hello .... (A) Manchester United, 29/12/73, D1, L 0-2
Town Farewell .... (H) Aston Villa, 21/9/85, D1, L 0-3
Appearances 500
Goals 11

A product of the fabled Portman Road youth system, George Burley marked George Best out of the game on his debut at Old Trafford, aged 17, in 1973. He made exactly 500 appearances in total and won the Player of the Year award in 1977/1978 and eleven caps for Scotland. He unfortunately missed the Uefa Cup final in 1981 due to damaged knee ligaments but led the club to Wembley success in 1999/2000 as manager and a return to the Premiership where they were to finish fifth and return to European football.

BILLY THE WIZ

Wing-wizard Billy Reed has the distinction of being Town's first player to receive international honours when he played for Wales against Yugoslavia in a 3-1 defeat in 1954. Born in Rhondda, his exceptional dribbling prowess saw him christened the 'Stanley Matthews' of the Third Division and he scored 46 goals in 169 starts before joining Swansea City.

OLD MAN BURNS

Goalkeeper Mick Burns, aged 43-years-old, became the oldest player to represent Ipswich, in a 2-2 draw at Gateshead in the FA Cup third round in 1952. Burns was an interesting character. He had already appeared in the FA Cup final for Preston North End in 1937 against a victorious Sunderland before joining Ipswich and started between the posts in Town's first ever professional game in 1938. He later saw action in Italy and North Africa during World War II and was to guest for Norwich City during that time. After making 168 appearances for Ipswich he retired and became caretaker at a school in Newcastle.

CUP MEMORIES

There are numerous competitions that Town have entered over the years which are now defunct: Full Members Cup, Anglo-Italian Cup, Willhire Cup and the Texaco Cup.

Full Members Cup 1986-92

The Full Members Cup was a short-lived supplementary cup competition for full members of the Football League; i.e. those belonging to the old First and Second Divisions. It was introduced in 1985 following the European ban on English clubs along with the Super Cup. However, it was never very popular, and was viewed as an irritating irrelevance by the top clubs who usually declined to enter, and by the football supporters in general who stayed away from matches in droves (although the crowds at the finals were quite creditable). Town's best performance in this multi-named tournament came in the 1986/87 season, the first season that they had entered. Having beaten Plymouth Argyle, Reading, Aston Villa and Manchester City in previous rounds they succumbed to Blackburn Rovers, 2-0, in the semi-final at Ewood Park.
Number of seasons entered: six. Best: semi-finalists 1986/87

Anglo-Italian Cup 1969-95

The original Anglo-Italian Cup grew out of the need to give Swindon Town some reward for winning the League Cup in 1969 (as a Third Division team they could not be admitted into the Fairs Cup). It was not a very successful competition and in 1975 it was abandoned, although the Anglo-Italian connection continued in the shape of a new tournament for semi-professional sides. In 1993 the idea of an Anglo-Italian Cup was revived to replace the discredited Full Members (ZDS) Cup. The new competition involved teams from the secondary divisions of the two countries (Football League Division One and Italian Serie B). It was a complete flop with most games, especially in Italy, attracting only minimal crowds and very little coverage. It managed to survive four seasons before disappearing into oblivion in 1996. The Blues' single foray into the Anglo-Italian tournament saw them top their group in the first stage only to be surprisingly beaten by Port Vale, 4-2 in the knock-out stage.
Number of seasons entered: one. Best: English semi-finalist 1995/96

MASTER AND APPRENTICE: GEORGE BURLEY LEADS HIS MEN TO A 1-0 WIN OVER NEWCASTLE UNITED IN 2001

PUNCH

Willhire Cup 1978-80

The Willhire Cup, named after sponsors Willhire (a local vehicle hire company), was created in 1978 to add a competitive edge to pre-season matches. Four of East Anglia's Football League sides, Town, Colchester, Cambridge United and Norwich competed in this league format tournament. Town were crowned the winners in 1978 and 1979, before the tournament finished in 1980.

Number of seasons entered: three. Best: winners 1978 and 1979

Texaco Cup 1971-75

The Texaco Cup was sponsored by the petrol company and involved clubs from England, Scotland, Northern Ireland and the Republic of Ireland who hadn't qualified for Europe. The Irish clubs withdrew after the 1971-72 competition due to political unrest and competed in a separate Texaco Irish Cup. Texaco withdrew their sponsorship in 1975 and were replaced by the Anglo-Scottish Cup. The Texaco Cup will forever hold a place in the hearts of Town fans of the era for the style in which Norwich City were beaten in the two-legged final of the 1972/73 competition. Town did not have an opportunity to defend the trophy due to Uefa Cup commitments the following season, having qualified for Europe several weeks earlier.

Number of seasons entered: one. Best: winners 1973

THE UNFORGETTABLE SEASON

The 1980-1981 season is etched in Portman Road folklore. Town finished the campaign as Uefa Cup winners, with a impressive run to the final that included a 4-1 away win at St. Etienne over Michel Platini, Johnny Rep and company. They also finished Division One runners-up and reached the FA Cup semi-final. The club's Player of the Year was Paul Cooper, while John Wark was elected Player of the Year by the PFA, with Frans Thijssen and Paul Mariner coming second and third respectively. Frans Thijssen was voted the Football Writers' Player of the Year, with Mick Mills, John Wark and Arnold Muhren finishing in second, third and sixth places, respectively. Wark finished with 36 league and cup goals and his 14 goals in the Uefa Cup equalled the record for most goals in European competition by one player in one season.

WE'VE GOT A FINNISH INTERNATIONAL...

Shefki Kuqi

Position ....Striker
Born .... Yugoslavia, November 10th 1976
Town Hello .... (A) Watford, 27/9/03, D1, W 2-1
Town Farewell .... (H) Hull City, 4/5/08, FLC, W 1-0
Town/Intl Appearances 92/7
Town/Intl Goals 32/2

An old-fashioned, bustling striker, Kuqi was signed by Joe Royle – initially on loan from Sheffield Wednesday in 2003 – and he scored a fine goal on his debut at Watford. His loan spell turned into a permanent move and the flying Finn, known for his trademark goal celebration dive, scored 32 goals in three different spells. His two Finland goals while he was under contract at Portman Road came in a 3-1 victory against Armenia.

WE'VE GOT A DUTCH INTERNATIONAL...

Arnold Muhren

Position .... Midfielder
Born .... Holland, June 2nd 1951
Town Hello .... (H) Liverpool, 22/8/78, D1, L 0-3
Town Farewell .... (H) Tottenham Hotspur, 17/5/82, D1, W 2-1
Town/Intl Appearances 214/7
Town/Intl Goals 29/2

A sublime midfielder, Muhren appeared as an unused substitute in two European Cup finals for Ajax before Bobby Robson made one of his greatest signings when he sealed Muhren's signature for £165,000 from Twente Enschede in 1978. A glittering Suffolk career saw him win the Uefa Cup before signing for Manchester United in 1982. He went on to win the FA Cup at Old Trafford in 1983 as well as the European Championship with Holland in 1988. As of June 2009, he is a youth coach at Ajax.

WELSH WONDERS

Six players have been capped for Wales while at Portman Road.

Billy Reed.................2 caps....................1954
Cyril Lea...................2 caps....................1965
Mick Hill...................2 caps....................1971
Geraint Williams.......2 caps..........1993-1995
Gavin Williams........1 cap.....................2005
Lewis Price...............3 caps..........2005-2006

PORTMAN ROAD LEGENDS

Billy Baxter

Position...Centre-half
Born..Edinburgh, April 23rd 1939
Town Hello............................(H) Norwich City, 27/12/60, D2, W 4-1
Town Farewell........(A) West Bromwich Albion, 23/1/71, FAC, D 1-1
Appearances...459
Goals...22

Baxter, who signed for Town aged 21, had just completed an engineering apprenticeship and was preparing for national service when Alf Ramsey came calling. He combined the start of his Town career with normal Army duties in the Royal Engineers at Aldershot, and a hectic travel schedule between the barracks, Portman Road and his home in Edinburgh. He won three league titles in Suffolk and made 131 consecutive league appearances before his long service was rewarded with a testimonial match against West Ham United in 1970. His departure from the club was tinged with sadness, however, after an article in a newspaper, attributed to him, had him berating the club after a game with Leeds United. He was unable to give a satisfactory explanation to new manager Bobby Robson and was suspended and relieved of his captaincy before joining Hull City.

PACKING THEM IN

The highest season average home attendance at Portman Road was in 1974/1975 when 25,775 flocked to watch the Blues on a regular basis.

WE'VE GOT AN ENGLISH INTERNATIONAL...

Trevor Whymark

Position ....Striker
Born .... Burston, May 4th 1950
Town Hello .... (A) Manchester City, 28/2/70, D1, L 0-1
Town Farewell .... (A) Bristol City, 3/2/79, D1, L 1-3
Town/Intl Appearances 335/1
Town/Intl Goals 104/0

Whymark scored 65 goals for Town's reserve and youth teams in the 1968-69 season before establishing himself as a regular in the 1972-1973 season. The season after he scored all four goals against Lazio in a Uefa Cup second round tie and later scored four in a 7-0 thumping of West Bromwich Albion in 1976-1977. His solitary England cap came against Luxembourg in 1977 in a 2-0 away win which also featured Paul Mariner and Kevin Beattie.

BANTAMS CLOSED

Ipswich destroyed Bradford City 5-1 in an FA Cup second round affair in December 1952 at Portman Road. The Bantams featured future England and Somerset cricket captain Brian Close in their ranks, who was 21 at the time and had made his Test debut against New Zealand three years earlier. He was 18 and is still the youngest ever player to represent England in a Test match; he went on to captain his country on seven occasions (six wins, one draw) and was renowned as one the bravest cricketers of all-time, playing against a fearsome West Indian pace attack at The Oval aged 45.

CROFT TAGGED

Left-back Gary Croft was given an excellent reception at Portman Road when Town crushed bottom club Swindon Town 3-0 in Division Two on January 15th 2000. He was the first professional footballer to play wearing an electronic tag after returning to action after four weeks in prison after admitting to a string of motoring offences. Croft paid his respects to the fans at the final whistle when he went to each end of the stadium to bow down in honour of their unwavering support.

SCORING FOR FUN

When The Blues won 2-1 at Leyton Orient in January 1954, they not only stayed seven points clear at the top of Division Three (South) but stretched a scoring record which covered an amazing 33 consecutive games. Goals from Tommy Parker and John Elsworthy extended a feat which is unlikely to be beaten for some time. Only two games of the run saw defeat – both 3-1 away losses.

1/5/1953	Aldershot (H) D3	2-1
19/8/1953	Walsall (A) D3	2-0
22/8/1953	Colchester United (H) D3	3-0
26/8/1953	Torquay United (H) D3	2-1
29/8/1953	Millwall (A) D3	2-1
2/9/1953	Torquay United (A) D3	1-1
5/9/1953	Leyton Orient (H) D3	3-1
9/9/1953	Gillingham (H) D3	6-1
12/9/1953	Reading (A) D3	1-3
16/9/1953	Gillingham (A) D3	1-1
19/9/1953	Southend United (H) D3	1-1
23/9/1953	Bournemouth (H) D3	2-1
26/9/1953	Brighton & Hove Albion (A) D3	2-1
30/9/1953	Bournemouth (A) D3	3-2
3/10/1953	Watford (H) D3	1-0
10/10/1953	Bristol City (A) D3	3-2
17/10/1953	Aldershot (H) D3	4-0
24/10/1953	Swindon Town (A) D3	2-1
31/10/1953	Walsall (H) D3	3-0
7/11/1953	Shrewsbury Town (A) D3	1-1
14/11/1953	Exeter City (H) D3	1-1
21/11/1953	Reading (H) FAC	4-1
28/11/1953	Norwich City (H) D3	1-1
5/12/1953	Queens Park Rangers (A) D3	1-3
12/12/1953	Walthamstow Avenue (H) FAC	2-2
16/12/1953	Walthamstow Avenue (A) FAC	1-0
19/12/1953	Colchester United (A) D3	2-1
25/12/1953	Coventry City (A) D3	3-1
26/12/1953	Coventry City (H) D3	4-1

2/1/1954	Millwall (H) D3	1-1
9/1/1954	Oldham Athletic (H) FAC	3-3
12/1/1954	Oldham Athletic (A) FAC	1-0
16/1/1954	Leyton Orient (A) D3	2-1

BUSBY'S BEAUTS

On January 25th 1958, two goals from Sir Bobby Charlton saw Manchester United beat Town 2-0 in front of 53,550 fans in the FA Cup fourth round. Sadly, it was the last time that the great 'Busby Babes' were to play at Old Trafford as the Munich air disaster happened less than two weeks later. Five players who played against Town that day – Roger Byrne, Eddie Colman, Duncan Edwards, Mark Jones and Tommy Taylor – were to tragically lose their lives when their plane crashed in blizzard conditions after an unscheduled refuelling stop in Munich on February 6th when returning from a European Cup match in Belgrade.

GOAL-GRABBING GREATS

There have been ten games since the club turned pro in 1936 in which a Town player has scored four or more goals. All have been at Portman Road. Southampton and West Bromwich Albion have each suffered twice.

Five in one game

Ray Crawford	Floriana 10-0	European Cup 1962
Alan Brazil	Southampton 5-2	Division One 1982

Four in one game

Gilbert Alsop	Aldershot Res 7-0	Southern League 1938
Fred Chadwick	Street 7-0	FA Cup 1938
Tom Garneys	Doncaster Rovers 5-1	Division Two 1954
Dermot Curtis	Stoke City 4-0	Division Two 1959
Ray Crawford	Southampton 5-2	League Cup 1967
Trevor Whymark	Lazio 4-0	Uefa Cup 1973
Trevor Whymark	West Brom 7-0	Division One 1976
Trevor Whymark	Landskrona Bois 5-0	Uefa Cup 1977
John Wark	Aris Salonika 5-1	Uefa Cup 1980
John Wark	West Brom 6-1	Division One 1982

BUILDING FOR THE FUTURE

The new Pioneer Stand (now Britannia Stand) was officially opened by Sir Stanley Rous when Town drew 1-1 with Manchester United in February 1983. The stand cost £1.4 million to build and seated 4,800. Due to constant development it now contains the directors' box, press area and houses a full-size Astroturf pitch behind it which is used for training throughout the week.

FIVE-STAR BRAZIL

Another memorable Portman Road evening encounter happened exactly 22 years later in 1982 when Scottish striker Alan Brazil scored every goal, and three in five minutes, as Ipswich crushed top-of-the-table Southampton 5-2 in Division One. England internationals Kevin Keegan, Alan Ball and Mick Channon all played for the Saints.

PORTMAN ROAD LEGENDS

Richard Naylor

Position ....Forward/defender
Born .... Leeds, February 28th 1977
Town Hello..........................(A) Sheffield United, 14/9/96, D1, W 3-1
Town Farewell ....(H) Bristol City, 10/12/08, FLC, W 3-1
Appearances... 374
Goals 40

Richard 'Bam Bam' Naylor became a Town legend due to his unstinting efforts to the Portman Road cause whether in defence or attack. Originally a centre-half, Naylor served for 14 years and suffered a host of injuries. His high point undoubtedly came playing a starring role and scoring in the 2000 Division One play-off final at Wembley. When George Burley was replaced by Joe Royle, Naylor was switched back to defence which improved his performances and ironically increased his goal scoring tally. He was given a testimonial against a Wembley 2000 XI in September 2006 which finished in a 3-3 draw. He joined boyhood favourites Leeds United in 2009 and was awarded the Elland Road captaincy.

BURLEY BATTERS THE ROBINS

Swindon Town would have been delighted when George Burley eventually left Ipswich Town as manager in 2002. His record at the County Ground was nothing short of unbelievable with 100% wins across four league games with 16 goals scored in total. The games were as follows:

W 4-0......................................April 12th 1997
W 2-0............................. December 28th 1997
W 6-0..April 3rd 1999
W 4-1.................................August 15th 1999

WORLD CUP WONDERS

Ten bits of World Cup finals trivia

1. Mick Mills captained his country in all five of England's games at Spain 1982.
2. John Wark's 29th minute goal for Scotland against New Zealand, in the same tournament, was the first by a Town player in the World Cup finals.
3. Wark's appearance in that game was also the first by a Town player in the finals.
4. Bontcho Guentchev has progressed the furthest in the finals, reaching the semi-final with Bulgaria at USA 1994.
5. Guentchev is the only Town player to have taken a spot kick in a penalty shoot-out and scored (in his country's 3-1 victory over Mexico).
6. Terry Butcher is the only Town player to have appeared in two World Cup finals (Spain and Mexico). He also played for England at Italia 90 while a Glasgow Rangers player.
7. The 2002 World Cup was the fourth to feature a Town player.
8. Matt Holland's appearance in Ireland's penalty shoot-out defeat by Spain (June 16th, 2002) was the 23rd World Cup finals game to feature a Town player.
9. Six Ipswich players where selected for Spain 82 (Mills, Mariner and Butcher for England, and Wark, Brazil and Burley for Scotland).
10. Ipswich are the only English club side to have provided the nation with a World Cup-winning manager

BUTCHER'S BLOODBATH

Giant centre-back Terry Butcher was famously remembered for receiving a horrific blood-stained gash playing for his country in a World Cup qualifier in Sweden. However, he received an even worse injury when Town defeated Luton 3-0 in the FA Cup in 1982. Going in for an unwinnable header, Butcher came out the worse and received a horrific nose injury which required 15 pints of blood via a post-match transfusion at London Hospital, where he was to spend two nights.

PORTMAN ROAD LEGENDS

Jason Dozzell

Position .... Midfielder
Born .... Ipswich, December 9th 1967
Town Hello .... (H) Coventry City, 4/2/84, D1, W 3-1
Town Farewell .... (A) Oxford United, 18/11/97, LC, W 2-1
Appearances 416
Goals 73

When Jason Irvin Winans Dozzell replaced Eric Gates and scored on his debut against Coventry City in 1984 he became Town's youngest ever scorer at the age of 16 years and 56 days. It marked the beginning of a memorable career which saw him play an instrumental part in leading the club to the Premiership under John Lyall in 1991/1992. He scored 15 goals that season from midfield and, after 13 years, moved to Tottenham Hotspur for £1,900,000 where injuries limited him to 99 appearances in five seasons. He joined Town for a second spell under George Burley before eventually managing local clubs Ipswich Wanderers and Leiston.

EURO GLORY

Four Town players have appeared in the European Championship finals: Paul Mariner and Mick Mills for England, Frans Thijssen for Holland and Claus Thomsen for Denmark. Town have had representatives at two of the finals. In Italy 1980 Paul Mariner and Mick Mills appeared for England while Frans Thijssen represented Holland. Danish midfielder Claus Thomsen appeared three times for his country in England in 1996.

PORTMAN ROAD LEGENDS

Mick Stockwell

Position	Midfield
Born	Chelmsford, February 14th 1965
Town Hello	(A) Coventry City, 26/12/85, D1, W 1-0
Town Farewell	(A) Stockport County, 15/4/00, D1, W 1-0
Appearances	610
Goals	44

Stockwell, an industrious midfielder who could play and perform admirably in many other positions, waited three years for his Town debut in 1985 but had made a lasting impact when he retired 15 years later. Ever present when Town won the Second Division title in 1991/1992 he won the club's Player of the Year award following their subsequent season in the Premiership in 1992/1993. After enjoying a spell as club captain and a testimonial against Sir Bobby Robson's Porto, Stockwell joined Colchester United where he won two Player of the Season Awards. Famously winning many Town fans good money after being overlooked by the bookmakers when named as an emergency striker at Wimbledon in a Premiership encounter, Stockwell's odds of 14-1 as first scorer were snapped up by the travelling faithful and he fulfilled the bargain with the opener in a 2-2 draw!

THE MEN WHO MANAGED THE TOWN

Jimmy Forsyth
Spell: September 1964 to October 1964
Honours: None
Overall Record: P 7; W 2 D 2 L 3 F 12 A 15

First team coach Jimmy Forsyth, assisted by Charlie Cowie and Kenny Malcolm, was responsible for team selection for the period between Jackie Milburn's departure and Bill McGarry's arrival a month later. His spell was notable for a 4-2 win at Middlesbrough which ended a run of 30 away games without a win. When Cyril Lea took over first team training in 1965, Forsyth began to work with the reserves before later becoming club physiotherapist. He spent over forty years in the game at Portman Road, Portsmouth, Gillingham and Millwall.

LOWES & HIGHS

David Lowe was a tremendous acquisition for the Town when John Duncan, newly appointed at the club, signed him from Wigan Athletic for £80,000 in June 1987. The small, attacking Scouser started off as an apprentice at Springfield Road after a recommendation from his teacher from his school league days, to then Wigan manager Harry McNally. Lowe made his first-team debut in October 1982 against Reading and in 1985 he would score in the Freight Rover Trophy final with a spectacular overhead kick to help his team beat Brentford 3-1. In June 1987, after playing 231 games for Athletic and tallying 53 goals, Lowe made the transfer to Town, making his debut in the 1987-88 season. He would go on to become the club's leading scorer for the campaign with 17 goals in 41 league games. The tireless striker would continue to find the net as well as picking up two England under-21 caps, having a tremendous strike against France disallowed at Highbury in April 1988. Lowe finished as leading marksman again in 1989-90 but two seasons later he was loaned out to Port Vale in 1992. In July of that year, Lowe left Town to join Leicester City for £250,000 after scoring 44 goals in 159 appearances. He signed off his Suffolk spell as a substitute for Steve Whitton as Town thrashed Tranmere Rovers 4-0 at Portman Road in November 1991. In a pre-season friendly against Borussia Mönchengladbach at Filbert Street he shattered his cheekbone but would eventually settle for the Foxes and become a regular first-teamer. In February 1994 he went back on loan at Port Vale. After a fruitful Leicester spell where he scored 23 goals in 77 starts, Lowe re-signed for Wigan Athletic for £125,000. In 1996-97, he celebrated his 300th league game for the club and his goal in the final game of the season would secure the Third Division title and promotion to Division Two. After collecting the club's supporters' and Player of the Year trophies, and a record tally of 83 goals, Lowe was released by Wigan in June 1999. After spells at Wrexham and Rushden & Diamonds he decided to retire as a player. In January 2009, whilst a coach at Derby County, Lowe was placed in temporary charge of a solitary game where his Derby team beat Manchester United 1-0 in the first leg of the League Cup semi-final at Pride Park Stadium. Nigel Clough officially started as manager the next day.

WE'VE GOT A BERMUDAN INTERNATIONAL...

Reggie Lambe

Position	Midfielder
Born	Bermuda, February 4th 1991
Town Hello	Not yet appeared
Town Farewell	Not applicable
Town/Intl Appearances	0/9
Town/Intl Goals	0/4

At the age of just 16, Lambe became the youngest ever Town full international when he appeared for Bermuda in a 2-1 defeat against St. Kitts and Nevis in December 2007. Although yet to appear for the first team, Lambe is a promising attacking midfielder who after numerous trial periods for the Academy in 2006/2007 signed as a youngster and settled at Portman Road. He announced his arrival on the international scene when he scored four goals in Bermuda's 7-0 mauling of St. Martin in August 2008.

PORTMAN ROAD LEGENDS

Frank Yallop

Position	Right-back
Born	Watford, April 4th 1964
Town Hello	(A) Everton, 17/3/84, D1, L 0-1
Town Farewell	(II) Port Vale, 23/1/96 AIC, L 2-4
Appearances	385
Goals	8

Genial Frank Yallop was a solid defender who filled in for the injured George Burley when making his debut at Goodison Park. He earned all of his 52 Canadian caps whilst at Portman Road including appearances during the qualifying stages of the World Cup in France 1998. Yallop won the Player of the Year award in the 1997/1998 season and scored two wonderful goals against Tottenham Hotspur and Manchester United in the club's first season in the Premiership. He joined Tampa Bay Mutiny in 1996 and later enjoyed managerial success in the MLS with San Jose Earthquakes. Frank also took charge of David Beckham for a spell when boss of LA Galaxy.

THE SOUTH LONDON EXPRESS

Wandsworth-born marksman Darren Bent was a rising star in the Town under-17 side that won the Academy League and made the semi-finals of the FA Youth Cup in 2001. His Blues debut was in a 3-1 win in Sweden over Helsingborg in the Uefa Cup second round which was televised live in England on BBC2 on a Thursday afternoon in November 2001. Town, 1-0 down at the break, stormed back to win 3-1 thanks to two late strikes from Marcus Stewart, as Bent replaced Richard Naylor with 15 minutes left in front of 2,500 travelling fans. In the same month, he scored his first goal for the club in a 4-1 defeat at Newcastle United in the League Cup after showcasing his dazzling pace when latching onto a long Jamie Clapham pass. He also netted his first Premiership goal in a 1-0 win against Middlesbrough in April 2002 just twenty seconds after replacing Martijn Reuser. In his next season, back in Division One, Bent tore up opposition rearguards with pace, skill and natural instincts and finished with 18 goals in all competitions, second in the scoring charts behind Pablo Counago. He then bagged 16 goals in 36 starts the following term although his goal against West Ham United in the 2003-04 play-off season was not enough to claim a place back in the Premiership. Bent and his team-mates finished disappointed again the following season against the same opponents at the same stage despite finishing with 19 goals in 50 appearances. Failure to reach the top flight meant that Town could not hold on to such a talent and he joined Charlton Athletic for £2.5 million in June 2005 after being tracked consistently by Addicks gaffer Alan Curbishley. His spell at Portman Road saw him plunder a magnificent 55 goals in only 110 starts and was great testament to the ability of the youth set-up. He was Charlton's top scorer for two consecutive seasons with 35 goals in 79 appearances and then in June 2007 he was snapped up by Tottenham Hotspur for a club record £16.5 million, which was a price tag that carried a huge burden. It also provided Portman Road with £2.58 million as Town had a 20% sell-on clause included in the transfer deal to Charlton. Despite being a supporter of Arsenal as a boy, Bent scored his first competitive goal for Spurs in a 4–0 home victory over Derby County in August 2007 and has 18 goals in 32 Premier League starts up to the end of the 2008/09 season.

PORTMAN ROAD LEGENDS

Ray Crawford

Position ....Forward
Born .... Portsmouth, July 13th 1936
Town Hello ....(A) Swansea City, 4/10/58, D2, L 2-4
Town Farewell .... (A) Wolves, 1/3/69, D1, D 1-1
Appearances 353
Goals..227

Ray Crawford was one of the most prolific goalscorers of his time, bettered
only by the likes of Jimmy Greaves and Roger Hunt. He netted on 227
occasions for Ipswich in 353 appearances and was the first English-born
player to score five goals in a single European game in the 10-0 home
win over Floriana in 1962. He scored 40 league goals as Town won the
Division Two championship in 1961 and 33 goals the following season
as Town lifted the Football League championship. Son of a professional
boxer, Crawford scored the club's first top flight hat-trick in a 5-2 win
against Chelsea soon after becoming the first Town player to win an
England cap against Northern Ireland at Wembley. He provided Bobby
Charlton with the pass for England's goal in a 1-1 draw. In April of the
following year, he again played for his country at Wembley and scored in
England's 3-1 success over Austria and scored both goals in the league-
championship clinching 2-0 victory against Aston Villa at Portman
Road on 28th April, 1962. All this after Crawford was reluctant to sign
for the club after watching his potential new employers at a game at
Leyton Orient in 1958 and not being impressed!

CARLISLE'S FINEST

Kevin Beattie, known as "The Beat", was a product of the Town youth
policy who went on to win nine full England caps and an FA Cup
winner's medal for the Blues. He was a huge favourite with the fans and
also won the PFA Young Player of the Year award in 1973. "The Beat"
scored against Scotland at Wembley in 1975 in a 5-1 thrashing, was one
of nine siblings, all born in Carlisle, and his father had turned down the
chance to play for Aston Villa as a goalkeeper.

THE BEAT: YOUNG DEFENDER KEVIN BEATTIE POSING FOR THE CAMERAS IN 1973

ROME RIOT

Town's Uefa Cup campaign in the 1973/1974 season was a journey to Real Madrid, Lazio and FC Twente before defeat to Lokomotiv Liepzig on penalties. The game in Rome, in which Town entered with a 4-0 first leg lead following a quartet of goals from Trevor Whymark, witnessed some revolting scenes at the final whistle as the game degenerated into a mass brawl. Ipswich players were chased off the pitch and literally kicked and punched down the tunnel and into the away dressing room. They stayed in there for a good hour after the game had finished. Manager Bobby Robson emerged to say to the press: "No Italian player can be excused. They acted like savages, animals. If any one of my players had acted even fractionally like that they would never be allowed even to wear the shirt of Ipswich Colts." Ipswich lost the game 4-2 on the night but had gone through 6-4 on aggregate.

PORTMAN ROAD LEGENDS

Terry Butcher

Position	Centre-half
Born	Singapore, December 28th 1958
Town Hello	(A) Everton, 15/4/78, D1, L 0-1
Town Farewell	(A) Sheffield Wednesday, 3/5/86, D1, L 0-1
Appearances	351
Goals	21

Terry Butcher spent his childhood in Suffolk after leaving Singapore where his father was stationed with the Royal Navy. Butcher, an incredibly courageous centre-back, famously turned down Norwich City before a superb career at Portman Road highlighted by monumental displays as Town became one of the top sides in the country. His brilliant header at FC Cologne in the Uefa Cup semi-finals sent Town through to the 1981 final and he went on to win 77 caps for England (45 of which he won while at Ipswich). After gaining further trophies at Glasgow Rangers, Butcher enjoyed managerial spells at Coventry City, Sunderland, Motherwell, Sydney, Brentford and Inverness as well as assisting his former team-mate George Burley with Scotland.

PALMER THE FARMER

Steve Palmer, born March 31st 1968, was one of the very few footballers who have joined professional football from Cambridge University. After obtaining a degree in software engineering, he signed for the club in the 1989 season, for nothing, following a typically energetic and hard-working display in the Varsity Match. Ironically, he was to make his Football League debut for Ipswich at Oxford United in September 1989, replacing Neil Thompson in a 2-2 draw. He only appeared in a couple more matches that season but in 1990-91, after a long period on the bench, he was finally given an extended run in the side. He scored his first goal for the club in a 1-1 draw at Portsmouth in December 1990. Palmer still struggled to cement a regular place in the Town side, despite appearing as a replacement for an injured Paul Goddard in the 1991-92 Second Division-winning campaign. The following season he suffered horrendous injury problems due to a problematic thigh which led to him joining Watford in September 1995 for £135,000. A loyal, hard-working player who enjoyed the respect of the Portman Road faithful, Palmer left for Vicarage Road after three goals in 131 Blues appearances. In Hertfordshire he soon became a mainstay of the side and his versatility proved to be a bonus in the 1997-98 campaign when he started a league match in every shirt number from 1 to 14 – an amazing feat which required a little assistance from Watford and England manager Graham Taylor. With promotion assured as Second Division champions, Palmer started the home match against AFC Bournemouth in goal, keeping a clean sheet for all of ten seconds before changing places with regular keeper, and former Town trainee, Alec Chamberlain. Palmer was voted the Hornets' Player of the Year in 1998-99 and was an ever present the following season and continued to serve Watford well until the end of the 2000-01 season when, after featuring in 262 games, he joined Queens Park Rangers. Promptly appointed captain, he was the club's only ever present in seasons 2001-02 and 2002-03, finally playing 101 consecutive league games. He was released in the summer of 2004 when he joined MK Dons and combined playing with coaching duties. Interestingly, Palmer played a first-class cricket match for a Cambridge University side, also containing future England captain Mike Atherton, against Lancashire in April 1987. He dismissed former England player Graeme Fowler lbw for 49 and scored 18 with the bat, before being bowled by Paul Allott.

WE'VE GOT A CANADIAN INTERNATIONAL...

Bruce Twamley

Position .... Midfielder
Born ....British Columbia, May 23rd 1952
Town Hello ....(A) Wolverhampton W, 9/3/74, D1, L 1-3
Town Farewell..........................(H) Leicester City, 29/3/75, D1, W 2-1
Town/Intl Appearances 2/7
Town/Intl Goals.. 0/0

Twamley worked his way up the ranks at Portman Road after signing as an amateur but left Suffolk after making only two appearances. He returned to Canada in 1975 to play for the Vancouver Whitecaps before joining New York Cosmos where he featured alongside the likes of Pele. Twamley won seven full international caps for the Maple Leafs whilst at Town but never appeared in a defensive display that featured a clean sheet.

PORTMAN ROAD LEGENDS

Roy Bailey

Position .... Goalkeeper
Born ....Epsom, May 26th 1932
Town Hello .... (A) Norwich City, 2/4/56, D3(S), L 2-3
Town Farewell..........................(A) Coventry City, 23/9/64, LC, L 1-4
Appearances 346

Roy Bailey was living in a caravan in Lewisham when Alf Ramsey signed him from Crystal Palace and with Larry Carberry, John Elsworthy, Ted Phillips and Jimmy Leadbetter remains one of the only players who have won First, Second and Third Division championship medals with the same club. He was evacuated to Somerset during the war and went to school in Weston-super-Mare but returned to his native Surrey at the age of 15. He arrived at Ipswich on the last day before the transfer deadline in March 1956 and he came into the league side in the Easter derby match with Norwich City at Carrow Road. He conceded two goals in the first three minutes, but despite such a disastrous start he soon displaced George McMillan as the Town's regular goalkeeper. Bailey's son Gary, who was born in Ipswich, went on to play for Manchester United and England.

YOU'RE OFF SON

Town have never had more than one player dismissed in a single game, although on nineteen occasions there have been multiple dismissals in a single match.

Sammy McCrory & John Cropley (Aldershot)............ Portman Road 1950
Colin Viljoen & Frank Munro (Wolves)........................ Portman Road 1973
John Wark & Charlie George (Derby) .... Portman Road 1977
Peter Withe & Colin Gibson (both Aston Villa) .... Portman Road 1984
Russell Osman & Simon Stainrod (QPR)........................Loftus Road 1985
Phil Whelan & Martin Keown (Arsenal)....................... Portman Road 1994
Ian Hughes & Andy Gray (Bury).................................... Portman Road 1997
Jamie Scowcroft & Craig Harrison (Middlesbrough).. Portman Road 1997
Eddie Youds & Nigel Pepper (both Bradford City) ..... Portman Road 1998
Andrew Legg & Andrew Bernal (both Reading)......... Portman Road 1998
Manu Thetis & Sean Flynn (West Brom)................... The Hawthorns 1999
Larus Sigurdsson & Matt Carbon (both West Brom). Portman Road 1999
Mike Whitlow & Robbie Elliott (both Bolton) .... Portman Road 2000
Joe Dolan & Steven Reid (both Millwall) .... Portman Road 2000
Matteo Sereni & Lee Marshall (Leicester)....................... Filbert Street 2001
Martin McIntosh & Julian Baudet (both Rotherham) Portman Road 2003
Jonathan Macken & Ben Watson (both C Palace)....... Portman Road 2005
Alex Bruce & Stephen Bywater (Derby C).................... Portman Road 2007
Jack Cork (Scunthorpe U) & Pablo Counago............... Glanford Park 2008

WHO'S THE PRIDE OF ANGLIA?

As of August 2015, Town and Norwich City have clashed 85 times in League encounters. Ipswich have the vastly superior record with 38 wins to Norwich's 32 while 15 games have ended in stalemate. In one of the most exciting local derbies ever, Town pipped City 4-3 at Carrow Road in front of nearly 30,000 fans in February 1968. Despite the hosts going 2-0 up after 28 minutes, the visitors roared back to lead 4-2 after 67 minutes thanks, mainly, to a wonderful hat-trick from South African-born midfielder Colin Viljoen. Viljoen had scored a hat-trick on his debut against Portsmouth the previous season and won two England caps, a Player of the Season award and scored 54 goals in 368 league and cup outings.

DESTRUCTION DERBY

Town crushed The Canaries 5-0 at Portman Road on Saturday February 21st 1998. The boys in blue outclassed their rivals thanks to a magnificent Alex Mathie hat-trick and a glorious double from Dutchman Bobby Petta.

MILLWARD OFF THE MARK

Doug Millward scored Town's fastest ever goal, after only ten seconds, in a 5-0 drubbing of Newport County in February, 1957. Ted Phillips, Neil Myles and another for Millward completed the scoring. Millward left Southampton and joined Town in 1956 where he won two titles. He scored 36 goals before managing St. Mirren and then coaching tennis in the United States. His ashes were scattered over the Solent in 2000 where he had been involved in an air-sea rescue operation while on National Service.

PORTMAN ROAD LEGENDS

Colin Viljoen

Position	Midfield
Born	Johannesburg, June 20th 1948
Town Hello	(H) Portsmouth, 25/3/67, D2 W 4-2
Town Farewell	(A) Aston Villa, 29/4/78, D1, L 1-6
Appearances	368
Goals	54

South African midfielder Viljoen had a remarkable first and last appearance for the Blues which sandwiched 368 outings over a decade. On his debut, with his side two down against Portsmouth after fifteen minutes, Viljoen announced himself on the scene with an incredible hat-trick which saw Town triumph 4-2. Viljoen went on to win two England caps and endeared himself to the locals with another stunning hat-trick over Norwich City in 1967/1968. In 1978, despite missing the majority of the season due to injury, Bobby Robson gave Viljoen a pre FA Cup final run-out at Villa Park instead of Roger Osborne who had played a big part in getting the club to Wembley. Town crashed to a horrendous 6-1 defeat and Osborne was reinstated to the team to become a Wembley hero. Viljoen left soon after for Manchester City then Chelsea before returning to South Africa.

VOLVO VANDALS

In March 1981, as 35,000 fans crammed into the City Ground, Town's new £65,000 Volvo executive coach was vandalised as the Blues earned a credible 3-3 draw with Nottingham Forest in the FA Cup quarter-final. The Blues exacted revenge with a 1-0 victory in the replay only three days later.

THE MEN WHO MANAGED THE TOWN

Bill McGarry
Spell: October 1964 to November 1968
Honours: Division Two Champions 1967/1968
Overall Record: P 196: W 80 D 62 L 54 F 323 A 272

Bill McGarry began his playing career at local club Port Vale before joining Huddersfield Town in 1951 and then winning four caps for England as a tough defender. He enjoyed managerial spells at Bournemouth and Watford before being appointed to the Portman Road hotseat in 1964, to turn around the club after the unsuccessful Jackie Milburn experiment. He took his abrasive style of play into management in Suffolk and focused on player strength and stamina – his sixth game in charge resulted in a 7-0 defeat of Portsmouth. He won the Second Division in 1968, his re-signing of legend Ray Crawford proved to be an inspiration, but months into the new campaign he walked out and joined Wolverhampton Wanderers, who he led to the Uefa Cup final in 1972 and won the League Cup with in 1974. Spells followed as manager of Saudi Arabia, Newcastle United and Wolves again before moving to South Africa where he died aged 77.

PACKED OUT AT PORTMAN ROAD

A Portman Road record crowd of 38,010 saw Ipswich and Leeds United slug out a drab goalless draw in the FA Cup sixth round. New Portman Stand extensions were in use for the first time to cram in an attendance unlikely to ever be beaten. It was the start of four titanic cup tussles between Town and the Whites in March that year. Town eventually triumphed 3-2 at Filbert Street in a third replay.

UEFA CUP FINAL 1981

First Leg – Wednesday 6th May 1981

Ipswich Town	3-0 (1-0)	AZ Alkmaar

Wark 28 (pen)
Thijssen 46
Mariner 56

Att: 27,532

Ipswich Town	AZ Alkmaar
1. Paul Cooper	1. Treytyl
2. Mick Mills (capt.)	2. Van Der Meer
3. Steve McCall	3. Spelbos
4. Frans Thijssen	4. Metgod
5. Russell Osman	5. Hovenkamp
6. Terry Butcher	6. Peters
7. John Wark	7. Jonker
8. Arnold Muhren	8. Arnst
9. Paul Mariner	9. Kist
10. Alan Brazil	10. Nygaard (Welzl)
11. Eric Gates	11. Tol

Ipswich swept aside an ultra-physical AZ 67 Alkmaar, the runaway champions of the Dutch league, to leave themselves with a great chance of winning the Uefa Cup. The Dutch leaders paid the price for trying to keep the score down rather than go on the attack and were far more interested in defending than entertaining with the tackles flying in as Paul Mariner and Eric Gates particularly suffered. However, Town stuck to their task sensibly and after 27 minutes Hovenkamp handled a fierce shot by Mariner. Adolf Prokop, the East German referee, had no hesitation in pointing to the spot and John Wark ran up and hammered home his 34th goal of the season. Whatever Bobby Robson said to his troops at the break worked as within 11 minutes of the second half the gap had widened to 3-0. The second came a mere 46 seconds into the second half when Thijssen, having seen Treytel save his effort, followed up to head the ball past the off-balance keeper. Ten minutes later, Alan Brazil worked his way into the Dutch penalty box and his low cross was glanced in nonchalantly by Mariner to set a packed Portman Road into raptures and the Blues on course for the second leg in Amsterdam.

THE BAIRD ESSENTIALS

Harry Baird, born in Belfast in 1913, was a wing-half who played 227 games for Town just after World War II and also represented Northern Ireland, Linfield, Manchester United and Huddersfield Town. During Baird's playing career there were, in effect, two Ireland teams, chosen by two rival associations. Both associations – the Northern Ireland-based IFA and the Irish Free State-based FAI – claimed jurisdiction over the whole of Ireland and selected players from the whole island. As a result several notable Irish players from this era played for both teams. However, each association challenged the selection policy of their rival and Baird found himself caught in the middle of one of several disputes. In May 1938 Baird, together with Jackie Brown and Walter McMillen, was one of three Northern Ireland-born players called up by the FAI XI to play in two friendlies against Czechoslovakia and Poland. However, the IFA objected and Baird subsequently received a telegram from the English FA ordering him not to accept the offer on the grounds he was not born in the Irish Free State. After Linfield, where he won an Irish League title and the Irish Cup, Baird was signed by Manchester United in January 1937 for a fee of £3,500. He joined a struggling side and could do little to prevent United from being relegated at the end of the 1936-37 season but during the following campaign he helped United gain promotion back to the First Division when he finished as their joint top goalscorer with 15 goals. Baird then joined Huddersfield Town in 1938 and while there helped them reach the semi-final of the FA Cup in 1939. During the Second World War, Baird served in the RAF and guested with several clubs, including his former club Linfield and the Blues, who he would eventually sign for when the war finished. Baird made his debut for Ipswich on August 31st 1946 in a 2-2 draw at Leyton Orient in Division Three (South) which was the opening game of the season. He missed only a couple of games as the club finished sixth. Baird was then an ever present the next season as Town moved up to fourth and was to keep his place for the next three seasons. Baird retired as a player during the 1951-52 season, making his final appearance at Crystal Palace on October 20th 1951 in a 3-1 defeat. He subsequently became a coach at Portman Road.

WE'VE GOT A DANISH INTERNATIONAL...

Claus Thomsen

Position ....Midfielder
Born ....Aarhus, Denmark, May 31st 1970
Town Hello ....(H) Bolton Wanderers, 21/9/94, LC, L 0-3
Town Farewell..................(A) Nottingham Forest, 4/1/97, FAC, L 0-3
Town/Intl Appearances 97/12
Town/Intl Goals.. 8/0

Thomsen, an elegant central midfielder signed for £200,000 from Aarhus, made his debut for Denmark whilst an Ipswich player, in a home game against Macedonia in April 1995. He impressed for Denmark at Euro 1996 and, despite attracting the attentions of the likes of Juventus, the midfielder ended up at Everton for £900,000 in January 1997 before later appearing for FC Copenhagen and VFL Wolfsburg.

WILLIAMSON THE WILDCARD

Referee Iain Williamson has the dubious honour of being the official who has sent off the most Town players. Amazingly, in only ten games he's taken charge of, Williamson has sent off four Town players, and two of the opposition. First up, he sent French defender Georges Santos to the stands in a 0-0 draw at Millwall in December 2003 and then Alex Bruce for fighting Steven Bywater in a 2-1 Town home win over Derby County in April 2007 (Bywater was also dismissed to an early bath). A dismal 2-1 defeat at Coventry City saw Williamson red card Tommy Miller in the dying minutes before he sent off Pablo Counago and Jack Cork for fighting when the Blues beat Scunthorpe United 2-1 at Glanford Park in March 2008. Panic when you see the Berkshire official in charge of future Ipswich clashes!

CLOUGH NOT KEANE

Roy Keane was an important part of the Nottingham Forest side that eventually went on to lose the 1991 FA Cup final to Tottenham Hotspur. However, in the third round, Keane's costly error led to Palace snatching a late equaliser which led to the Town gaffer being punched in the face by Brian Clough in the dressing room after the game.

THE MEN WHO MANAGED THE TOWN

Sir Bobby Robson
Spell: January 1969 to May 1982
Honours: FA Cup winners 1978;
Uefa Cup winners 1981; Texaco Cup winners 1973;
Division One runners-up 1980/81 and 1981/82;
FA Youth Cup winners 1973 and 1975.
Overall Record: P 709: W 316 D 173 L 220 F 1031 A 814

Undoubtedly one of the game's best managers and a universally loved character, Robson was born in Durham in 1933 and had a distinguished playing career with Fulham and West Bromwich Albion, making almost 600 appearances. He also collected 20 England caps and scored four goals. Despite interest from Arsenal and Southend United, he coached the Vancouver Royals in Canada before rejoining Fulham as manager in 1968. He was sacked by the west London club after just 18 months; he found out not via the club, but from an *Evening Standard* billboard outside Putney Bridge station proclaiming "Robson Out". He was then appointed Town manager in January 1969 after being spotted by Town director Murray Sangster scouting for Chelsea when Ipswich lost to Nottingham Forest at Portman Road. Four mediocre seasons followed, which included calls from a section of supporters for Robson to be sacked, but the board stayed patient and unbelievable success was to follow. He guided Town to the FA Cup in 1978 and the Uefa Cup in 1981 and only brought in 14 players from other clubs during his tenure, mainly focusing on the club's fabled youth set-up. Appointed manager of England in 1982, Robson took the nation to their best finish in a World Cup since 1966 when they reached the Italia 90 semi-finals. He resigned not long after and won domestic titles with both PSV Eindhoven and Porto and the Cup Winners' Cup with Barcelona. He then joined bottom-of-the-table Newcastle United in 1999, winning his first game in charge 8-0 against Sheffield Wednesday before being sacked in 2004. On May 5th 2008, during the 30th anniversary celebrations of the 1978 FA Cup win, Robson was granted the Freedom of Ipswich by the Lady Mayor and a statue of him was unveiled behind the Cobbold Stand in 2002. Robson beat cancer five times in his later life, before losing his brave 17-year battle on Friday 31st July, at the age of 76.

PORTMAN ROAD LEGENDS

Allan Hunter

Position .... Centre-half
Born .... Sion Mills, June 30th 1946
Town Hello .... (H) Leicester City, 11/9/71, D1, L 1-2
Town Farewell .... (A) Shrewsbury Town, 14/2/82, FAC, L 1-2
Appearances 355
Goals 10

Possibly Town's best ever centre-half, and certainly the most popular, Allan Hunter was signed from Blackburn Rovers for £60,000 in 1971 and went on to make over 350 appearances in the blue and white of Ipswich; first in a central defensive pairing with Derek Jefferson and then, most famously, with Kevin Beattie, a partnership christened "Bacon and Eggs" by Bobby Robson. An FA Cup winner in 1978, Big Al also made 47 appearances for his native Northern Ireland while a Town player, and 53 in all for his country. His nephew, Barry Hunter, managed Rushden & Diamonds in 2005 before joining Norwich City as a scout while Glenn Roeder was in charge. As the song famously goes: "Six Foot Two, Eyes of Blue, Allan Hunter's after you…"

PROGRAMMED IN

Town's 2-0 defeat of Essex-based Old Parkonians in front of 2,000 fans in the Southern Amateur League on February 16th, 1924 witnessed the first appearance of a programme at Portman Road. The goalscorers that day were Fenn and Gathercole.

LET THERE BE LIGHT

The floodlights at Portman Road were officially opened by Lady Blanche Cobbold on Tuesday, February 16th 1960 in a 4-0 friendly defeat of Arsenal. Each tower was 100 feet high and held 30 lights with the whole cost borne by the Supporters' Association. Ted Phillips, Ray Crawford (2) and Doug Millward scored the goals in front of a crowd of 15,835 fans.

UEFA CUP FINAL 1981

Second Leg – Wednesday 20th May 1981

AZ Alkmaar   4-2 (3-2)   Ipswich Town
Welzl 6   *Frans Thijssen 3*
Metgod 25   *John Wark 42*
Tol 40
Jonker 74   Att: 28,500

Ipswich flew home with the Uefa Cup in the bag after memorable scenes at the Olympic Stadium, Amsterdam. Town survived a battling AZ performance who battled to the bitter end of the second leg of the final attempting to wipe out the three-goal deficit from the first leg. An amazing tie saw two goals in the first seven minutes with Town scoring the first when Thijssen half-volleyed home a Gates corner. Early goals, when they are scored in the away leg, are supposed to be invaluable but the Dutch side stormed back as Ipswich became complacent and soon after Welzl headed home a cross from Metgod. In the 25th minute Alkmaar deservedly moved in front, with Metgod heading a cross from Peters firmly past Cooper and the crowd, sensing that AZ might yet turn the game around despite the defeat at Portman Road, at last got behind their players. However, when Wark hooked home Muhren's corner kick on 31 minutes after a flick on by Mariner, it seemed AZ's task was impossible. But they didn't give up the fight. In the 40th minute they regained the lead on the night when Tol drove home past Cooper after Jonker nodded down the influential Metgod's cross. With 45 minutes left in the tie, and Ipswich leading 5-3 on aggregate, Alkmaar roared forward ceaselessly in search of more goals although 'Super' Paul Cooper dealt safely with efforts from Kist and Nygaard and then made a magnificent save from Welzl's header. The hosts finally broke through in the 73rd minute when Jonker hammered home a marvellous free kick, but despite incessant pressure the Town defence held out. The Blues had won their first and only European trophy to cap a never-to-be-forgotten night for the club.

AZ Alkmaar: Treytel; Reynders, Spelbos, Metgod, Hovenkamp, Peters, Jonker, Arntz, Welzl (Talan), Nygaard, Tol (Kist).

Ipswich Town: Paul Cooper; Mick Mills (capt.), Steve McCall, Frans Thijssen, Russell Osman, Terry Butcher, John Wark, Arnold Muhren, Paul Mariner, Alan Brazil, Eric Gates. No subs.

THE JOY OF JOHNSON

Gavin Johnson, born in Stowmarket in October 1970, made his Football
League debut for Town against Barnsley in a 2-0 win at Portman Road in
February 1989, just days after signing pro forms. Though he played only
sporadically over the next couple of seasons, he finally came to the fore in
1991-92, appearing in 42 games during the championship-winning campaign
under John Lyall. Originally a central defender, he was switched to the left side
of midfield and it was his goals in the last two games of the season that clinched
the title for the Blues. The first of those was at Oxford United's Manor Ground
in a 1-1 draw which clinched the title and sparked joyous scenes. In the next
game, as the trophy was paraded at Portman Road, he scored a cracker in a
3-1 win over Brighton & Hove Albion in front of 26,803 fans. The very next
season he had the honour of scoring Town's first-ever Premier League goal in
a 1-1 draw with Aston Villa on the opening day. He missed just two games
in 1992-93 but was unfortunate to pick up a knee injury during the final
match against Nottingham Forest when his studs got caught in a hole on the
Portman Road turf. Unable to win back his place on a regular basis, he joined
Luton Town on a free transfer after 160 games and 16 goals in Suffolk. After
a brief stay he signed for Wigan Athletic in December 1995 for £15,000.
The industrious Johnson proved he could play anywhere on the left flank,
and score some magnificent goals, especially from dead-ball positions. After
helping Wigan Athletic win the Third Division championship in 1996-97,
he again found his time chequered by groin problems and he was released in
the summer of 1998. After a short spell with Dunfermline Athletic, he joined
Colchester United and helped the Layer Road club maintain their Second
Division status. He was a permanent fixture until the second half of the 2001-
02 season when he suffered a broken leg at Port Vale. On returning to the side
he suffered another setback which required an operation and he spent a year
on the sidelines. After being released by Colchester in 2005 he had a brief spell
with Boston United, before spending a season with Northampton Town and
then Oxford United. In 2007 he returned to Suffolk to play for Bury Town.

MARINER THE MAGICIAN

March 30th 1977 saw Paul Mariner make his England debut as a second-half
replacement for Joe Royle in a 5-0 thrashing of Luxembourg in a Wembley World
Cup qualifier. He won 33 caps while at Portman Road and scored 14 goals.

THE MEN WHO MANAGED THE TOWN

Bobby Ferguson
Spell: August 1982 to May 1987
Honours: None
Overall Record: P 258: W 97 D 61 L 100 F 335 A 323

Robert Burnitt 'Bobby' Ferguson was a tough-tackling full-back from a footballing family who saw service with Newcastle United, Derby County, Cardiff City and Newport County. After a torrid spell as Newport County boss, he linked up with Robson at Portman Road in 1971 and coached the youngsters to two Youth Cup wins in 1973 and 1975 before replacing England-bound Robson as manager in 1982. He resigned at the end of the 1986/1987 season following Town's failure to gain promotion back to Division One after relegation the preceding season and was the first manager to be sacked by Ipswich Town.

DIB DIB DIB, DUNK DUNK DUNK

During half-time in Town's 1-0 Division One home win over Coventry City in 1982, members from 9th Ipswich Deben Cubs had a brew-up in the centre circle as part of a cub's competition to make tea in unusual places. City had future Town striker Steve Whitton in their line up.

HAT-TRICK HERO

Ipswich moved towards the summit of the First Division as they despatched Norwich City 4-2 at Portman Road on Easter weekend in 1980. The game witnessed John Wark's first Blues hat-trick – he completed the treble with a last-minute penalty.

IT ONLY TAKES A SECOND

Despite a 4-1 Premiership reverse at Arsenal, bubble-permed marksman Ian Marshall's strike prompted mass celebrations amongst the visiting Town fans at Highbury. In a miserable season, it was Town's first goal in 675 minutes of trying which also ran over seven consecutive league defeats.

WE'VE GOT AN ENGLISH INTERNATIONAL...

Richard Wright

Position ....Goalkeeper
Born ....Ipswich, November 5th 1977
Town Hello ....(H) Coventry City, 6/5/95, PL W 2-0
Town Farewell.. current player
Town/Intl Appearances 340/1
Town/Intl Goals.. 0/0

Ipswich-born Wright appeared once for the national team whilst on the books of the club in a friendly win in Malta in 2000. It proved to be an eventful day for the Suffolk stopper. He conceded a penalty which was converted but ordered to be taken again due to encroachment. The second kick hit the post and rebounded back into the net off Wright's head to register as an own-goal. With England 2-1 up, Wright conceded another penalty but this time saved it to register a victory for the visitors.

PORTMAN ROAD LEGENDS

Tommy Parker

Position .... Wing-half/inside-forward
Born .... Hartlepool, February 13th 1924
Town Hello ....(A) Watford, 3/11/45, D3(S), L 3-4
Town Farewell............................... (H) Millwall, 25/8/56, D3(S), L 0-2
Appearances 465
Goals...92

Thomas Roberston Parker 'guested' for Town during the 1945/1946 season while based at Shotley while he served in the Royal Navy. After establishing himself in the side, Parker missed just one game in each of seasons 1950/1951, 1951/1952 and 1952/1953 before being an ever-present when the club won the Third Division (South) title in 1953/1954. He broke the club's scoring record with 30 goals in league and cup football in the 1955/1956 season but soon lost his place to prolific poacher Ted Phillips the following campaign. Parker's appearance record was the club record until overhauled by Mick Mills and he worked for the club's Development Association from 1965 for two decades on retirement.

THE WRIGHT STUFF: ENGLAND'S RICHARD WRIGHT ON HIS DEBUT IN MALTA, 2000

THE MEN WHO MANAGED THE TOWN

John Duncan
Spell: June 1987 to May 1990
Honours: None
Overall Record: P 161: W 73 D 29 L 59 F 237 A 214

Signed by local club Dundee at 17, John Duncan won a Scottish League Cup medal in 1973, and after scoring 42 goals in a single season, joined Tottenham in 1974 for £160,000. Injury cut short his Spurs career, although he did manage to score 62 goals in just 120 appearances, joining Derby County in 1978. He had a spell managing Scunthorpe United and won a Fourth Division championship at Chesterfield before joining Town in 1987, replacing Bobby Ferguson. Three mid-table finishes saw him dismissed in 1990 when he rejoined Chesterfield and led them to the FA Cup semi-final in 1997. As of June 2009, he was managing the Loughborough University non-league side in the Midland Combination Premier Division.

STONEWALL'S AMAZING GAME

Goalkeeper John 'Stonewall' Jackson marked his only Ipswich game with a 2-1 midweek home win over mighty Manchester United in 1982. He was signed due to a glut of injuries at the age of 40 and left Town to join Hereford United where he eventually settled down after football to install blinds. Jackson was nicknamed 'Stonewall' by Crystal Palace supporters after a successful career at Selhurst Park covering eight seasons.

LYALL'S LOVELIES

A trip to Oxford United in April 1992 saw the Blues book a place in the inaugural Premier League the following season. A 1-1 draw at Oxford United cemented promotion from Division Two, Gavin Johnson levelling an earlier strike from future Town boss Jim Magilton at The County Ground. The point ensured memorable scenes at the final whistle as champagne-drenched players, led by hulking centre-back Phil Whelan, celebrated with over 2,000 visiting fans long into the night as the club celebrated its first honour in eleven years.

BETTER LUCK NEXT TIME

On Monday 7th June, 1937 the club initially tried to join the Football League at the end of a successful 1936-37 season, which they had ended as champions of the Southern League, winning the title by five clear points. Town, with 24 votes, were unsuccessful with their first application to play in the Football League after Exeter City (40 votes) and Aldershot City (34 votes) were re-elected to the Third Division (South) instead.

THE MEN WHO MANAGED THE TOWN

John Lyall
Spell: May 1990 to December 1994
Honours:
Division 2 Champions 1991/92
Overall Record: P 231: W 77 D 75 L 79 F 291 A 308

A talented left-back, John Lyall was a rising star at West Ham United before having to cruelly retire due to a knee injury aged 23. He rose through the coaching ranks at Upton Park and after being appointed boss won the FA Cup in 1975 and 1980. Sacked in 1989 after relegation to Division Two, Lyall arrived at Portman Road in 1990 and quickly rebuilt a team which he led to the Division Two title in 1991/1992. He took the club to fourth in the newly conceived Premiership before a dip in form almost led them to relegation (they were saved by Mark Stein's goal for Chelsea against Sheffield United on the final day). However, in December 1994, with the club at the foot of the table he was sacked. In 2006, he died suddenly of a heart attack in Tattingstone, Suffolk aged 66.

KING COLE WALLOPS TOWN

It was a day to forget for Blues followers, as Andy Cole scored five times, and future Ipswich manager Roy Keane netted, as Ipswich suffered their joint worst away defeat – and Manchester United their biggest win in a century – in a 9-0 Premiership encounter at Old Trafford in March 1995.

KUMBAYA MY LORD

A slippery striker with lightning pace, Chris Kiwomya followed his brother Andy into league football when he joined Town as a trainee in the summer of 1996. He had to wait a further 18 months before making his bow as a replacement for Neil Woods in a 1-1 draw against Bradford City at Portman Road in September 1988. He was to score the first of 64 Town career goals months later as the Blues smashed a sorry Walsall outfit 4-2 at Fellows Park in Division Two in January 1989. Despite the early promising signs, Kiwomya did not become a regular until the 1990-91 season in which he finished with a flourish and he topped the goalscoring charts with 12 goals in 39 starts. This was due mainly to manager John Lyall transforming him into a central striker, from a winger, and developing a telepathic partnership with Jason Dozzell. Although overlooked for England Youth and under-21 honours – despite being an unused substitute against Germany and suffering a torn thigh muscle days before playing Turkey – Kiwomya was a regular in the side which won the Second Division championship in 1991-1992, leading the way with 16 league goals and another three in cup competitions. He made a superb impact in the Premier League in 1992-1993 and also scored a sublime hat-trick against Wigan Athletic in a 4-0 Portman Road victory in the League Cup that season. As well as being leading scorer for three consecutive seasons from 1990-91 to 1992-93, the Huddersfield-born man showed fine confidence and awareness in his all-round play which led Arsenal manager George Graham to pay a fee of £1.25 million to take him to Highbury in January 1995, alongside John Hartson. Kiwomya had made 271 appearances for the Tractor Boys in just over six years. At the end of the 1995-96 season Kiwomya had scored three league goals in 14 league games but he was never to appear for the Gunners again. Troubled by injuries and a loss of form, he had loan spells with Le Havre and Selangor of Malaysia in 1997 before starting the 1998-99 season with Queens Park Rangers. After three seasons at Loftus Road, scoring 30 goals in 96 games, which included a goal against Town in a 3-1 Suffolk defeat for the Londoners in 1999, he went on to join Danish club Aalborg. Unsuccessful trials at Grimsby Town and Sheffield United saw him hang up his boots and he finally ended up coaching at Arsenal before joining Town in 2009 as a development coach.

PORTMAN ROAD LEGENDS

Russell Osman

Position	Centre-half
Born	Repton, February 14th 1954
Town Hello	(H) Chelsea, 3/9/77, D1, W 1-0
Town Farewell	(H) West Ham, 17/5/85, D1, L 0-1
Appearances	385
Goals	21

Russell Osman – the son of Rex who played for Derby County and was later to manage the Centre Sport restaurant at Portman Road – formed a formidable defensive partnership with Terry Butcher under the stewardship of Bobby Robson. After winning an FA Youth Cup medal in 1975, Osman was unlucky to not make an appearance in the 1978 FA Cup-winning team after performing notably that term. After winning a Uefa Cup medal in 1981 and eleven caps for England – he made his debut against Australia in Sydney alongside Butcher, Brian Talbot and Paul Mariner in a 2-1 victory – Osman joined Leicester City for £240,000 and then Southampton. He later managed Bristol City and Cardiff City before joining Exeter City as assistant manager and appearing as a pundit on Eurosport.

WASHED AWAY

On a truly miserable weekend for Suffolk, Town travelled back from a 4-1 stuffing at Torquay United in Division Three (South) on Saturday January 30th 1953. Following a long journey back from Devon by train, they found themselves marooned at Ipswich Station for five hours due to extensive flooding along the east coast. A severe North Sea storm that Saturday night was one of the most devastating natural disasters ever recorded in the UK. Over 1,600 km of coastline was damaged, and sea walls were breached forcing 30,000 people to be evacuated from their homes while 24,000 properties were seriously damaged. Thirty-eight people died at Felixstowe when wooden prefabricated homes in the West End area of the town were flooded. In Essex, Canvey Island was inundated with the loss of 58 lives, and a further 37 died when the seafront village of Jaywick near Clacton was flooded. The total death toll on land that night was estimated at 307.

THE MEN WHO MANAGED THE TOWN

Paul Goddard/John Wark
Spell: December 1994
Honours: None
Overall Record: P 3: W 0 D 2 L 1 F 4 A 7

Two Blues legends, Paul Goddard and John Wark, were put in caretaker charge of first team affairs at Portman Road for the three Premiership games played between John Lyall's departure and George Burley's arrival from Colchester United. Goddard, who won one England cap, was signed by Lyall and had been an influential figure as Town had won the Second Division title two years previously. He scored 15 goals in 109 first-team outings and went on to assist Glenn Roeder at West Ham United. He now lives in Suffolk working in football agency management.

DEBUT DELIGHT

Players who have scored on their Town debut in the 21st century:

Marcus Stewart v Barnsley .... 2-1 (A) Division One 2000
Martijn Reuser v Fulham .... 1-0 (H) Division One 2000
Shefki Kuqi v Watford .... 2-1 (A) Division One 2003
Darren Currie v QPR .... 4-2 (A) Championship 2004
David Unsworth v Sheffield U .... 2-0 (A) Championship 2005
Nicky Forster v Cardiff City .... 1-0 (H) Championship 2005
Gavin Williams v Coventry City .... 1-1 (A) Championship 2005
Ricardo Fuller v Leicester City .... 2-0 (H) Championship 2006
Kevin Lisbie v Preston North End .... 1-2 (H) Championship 2008
DJ Campbell v Cardiff .... 1-2 (H) Championship 2012
Noel Hunt v Charlton .... 1-0 (A) Championship 2014

PRESTON THE PROFESSIONALS

In 1892, Preston North End became the first professional club to play at Portman Road. A Suffolk County side, including three Town men in Notcutt, Haward and Kent, were no match for North End – one of the top teams of the era. The Suffolk side were defeated 3-0 by the Lillywhites.

SUPER STEWART: BRISTOLIAN MARCUS STEWART WAS A BIG HIT AT PORTMAN ROAD

RAZOR PLIGHT

Saturday March 25th 1972 was a dismal day for Town. They returned to Suffolk after a 1-0 defeat in Division One at Leicester City after manager Bobby Robson had his electric razor stolen from the dressing room as the Blues went down to a Dave Tomlin strike.

THE MEN WHO MANAGED THE TOWN

George Burley
Spell: December 1994 to October 2002
Honours: Division One play-off winners 1999/2000
Overall Record: P 413: W 188 D 96 L 129 F 620 A 497

George Burley was born in Cumnock, Scotland in 1956 and joined Town as a teenager making 500 first team appearances over a 14 year period before joining Sunderland in 1985. He won the FA Cup in 1978 with Town and marked George Best out of the game at Old Trafford on his Blues debut, aged 17, in 1973. Capped by Scotland 11 times at senior level, he rejoined as boss in 1994 from Colchester United and guided Town back to the Premiership via a Division One play-off final victory at Wembley in 2000. A fifth-place finish the following season, and qualification for the Uefa Cup for the first time since 1982, saw Burley voted Manager of the Year. Relegation followed, though, in 2002 and following a poor start to the 2002/03 season he was sacked before having spells as a manager at Derby County, Hearts and Southampton. He is the current manager of Scotland.

END OF AN ERA

Saturday April 24th 1963 was Alf Ramsey's final game in charge of Town before joining England as manager. It ended in a 2-1 victory over Burnley at Portman Road and goals by strike duo Ray Crawford and Ted Phillips brought the curtain down on Ramsey's reign in some style. Alf Ramsey won three championships in his Portman Road spell and his final season witnessed the club's first venture into Europe. A 14-1 aggregate win over Maltese club Floriana was followed by defeat to AC Milan in the European Cup.

THE MEN WHO MANAGED THE TOWN

Tony Mowbray
Spell: October 2002
Honours: None
Overall Record: P 4: W 1 D 1 L 2 F 5 A 7

Tony 'Mogga' Mowbray acted as caretaker manager for four games during the period following the sacking of George Burley and the appointment of Joe Royle in October 2002. An outstanding central defender with both Middlesbrough and Ipswich, many fans wanted Mowbray to get the job full-time but he was pipped at the post by Royle. Mowbray made 162 first-team outings and scored eight goals while at Portman Road and captained the club to their infamous 4-2 victory over Barnsley in the Wembley play-off final. He managed Hibernian, with Mark Venus as his assistant, and then West Bromwich Albion where he won the Championship title in 2007/2008.

PROFESSIONAL FOOTBALL ARRIVES IN SUFFOLK

On May 1st, 1936 perhaps the most significant meeting in the club's history convened at the Town Hall during which it was agreed that Ipswich Town Football Club would turn professional thereby bringing to a close the club's strongly-defended links to the amateur game that stretched back to 1878. This followed a turbulent few months during which a group of local businessmen, led by 21-year-old Leonard P. Thompson, threatened to form a new pro club 'Ipswich United' that would compete in the Southern League, play their games at the old Suffolk Greyhound Stadium on London Road, and hence threaten the seniority, and perhaps the very survival, of Ipswich Town FC. The meeting saw a resolution passed to amalgamate Ipswich Town FC and Ipswich United FC and Ipswich Town Football Club Ltd was formed and professional football was to finally arrive at Portman Road.

POORLY PORT VALE

As of August 2009, Town's home league record against Port Vale read: P 16; W 15, D 1, L 0. They did lose at home to the Valiants 1-0 in September 1945, though this is not included in the club's official records.

WE'VE GOT A DUTCH INTERNATIONAL...

Frans Thijssen

Position .... Midfield
Born .... Holland, January 23rd 1952
Town Hello .... (A) Derby County, 28/2/79, D1, W 1-0
Town Farewell .... (A) Norwich City, 4/5/83, D1, D 0-0
Town/Intl Appearances 170/10
Town/Intl Goals 16/2

A former teammate of Arnold Muhren at Twente Enschede, Bobby Robson raided the Dutch outfit again in 1979 to sign the left-footed midfield genius for £200,000. Thijssen was capped ten times for Holland whilst a Town player and scored twice. He scored in both legs of the club's 1981 Uefa Cup triumph and won the Football Writers' Association Footballer of the Year that season. He was only the second foreigner to win the accolade after Manchester City's goalkeeper Bert Trautmann in 1956.

WE'VE GOT AN ICELANDIC INTERNATIONAL...

Hermann Hreidarsson

Position .... Defender
Born .... Iceland, July 11th 1974
Town Hello .... (A) Tottenham Hotspur, 19/8/00, PL, L 1-3
Town Farewell .... (H) Stoke City, 8/3/03, D1, D 0-0
Town/Intl Appearances 128/16
Town/Intl Goals 3/1

A gigantic defender, Hreidarsson was effective either flying down the left flank or as a more traditional centre-half. The Icelandic legend was signed by George Burley for £4,000,000 from Wimbledon after playing for Iceland two days before. He made his debut for the Blues at White Hart Lane the day after signing and was capped 16 times by his country, netting once, before his transfer to Charlton Athletic in 2003 for £900,000.

LINIGHAN THE LEADER

David Linighan, the son of Brian, who played for Darlington in 1958 and whose brother, Andy, also joined Hartlepool United from Smiths Dock, made his league debut at the age of 17 against Bradford City in 1982. For a long while he played in the shadow of Andy and it was not until 1985-86 that he held down a regular place. He remained at Victoria Park for four years, making close to 100 league appearances for the club impressing Arthur Cox enough for Derby County to pay £30,000 for his signature. After only four months and no appearances, he was sold to Shrewsbury Town for £3,000. He missed only three matches in 18 months at Gay Meadow and, with Town looking to replace Ian Cranson following his move to Sheffield Wednesday, they took a punt by signing Linighan for £300,000 in June 1988. Linighan had made 65 league appearances for the Shrews and scored one goal. It was a gamble well worth taking as Linighan soon became a fixture in central defence and in 1990-91 he had a fantastic season as the club's captain, which was recognised by the Suffolk fans when he scooped the Player of the Year trophy. Linighan went on to play a sterling role in their Second Division championship campaign under John Lyall in 1991-92 until he was injured in a home game against Barnsley, which ruled him out for the rest of a successful season. Linighan again showed his inner strength to continue to be a model of defensive effectiveness in the Premiership and had played 328 games and scored 13 goals before joining Blackpool for £80,000 in November 1995 after a short loan spell at Bloomfield Road. Despite beginning his last season with the Blues on a weekly contract and losing the captaincy as a result, Linighan did recover the armband after fine displays in an overworked defence. After chalking up 100 league appearances for the Tangerines under three managers – Sam Allardyce, Nigel Worthington and Gary Megson – Linighan had a brief spell north of the border with Dunfermline Athletic before signing for Mansfield Town. He was a stalwart at the middle of the Stags defence until he broke his wrist towards the end of the 1999-2000 campaign. Freed by Mansfield, he then played non-league football for Southport before turning out for Chester City and Hyde United before retiring. Brother Andy also had a fine career and scored the winning goal for Arsenal against Sheffield Wednesday in the 1993 FA Cup final.

WE'VE GOT AN IRISH INTERNATIONAL...

Matt Holland

Position	Midfielder
Born	Bury, April 11th 1974
Town Hello	(A) Queens Park Rangers, 9/8/97, D1, D 0-0
Town Farewell	(A) Derby County, 4/5/03, D1, W 4-1
Town/Intl Appearances	314/33
Town/Intl Goals	45/4

An Ipswich Town legend, Holland went on to become one of the finest leaders Portman Road has witnessed after signing from AFC Bournemouth for £800,000 in 1997. He led the club into the Premiership and was also to feature impressively for his country in the 2002 World Cup finals in Japan – scoring a fine goal against Cameroon as well as captaining his nation against Scotland and Norway whilst on Ipswich's books. He joined Charlton Athletic for £750,000 in 2003 where he has become a firm favourite.

WE'VE GOT A WELSH INTERNATIONAL...

Cyril Lea

Position	Defender
Born	Moss, August 5th 1934
Town Hello	(H) Charlton Athletic, 21/11/64, D2, D 1-1
Town Farewell	(A) WBA, 23/4/69, D1, D 2-2
Town/Intl Appearances	123/2
Town/Intl Goals	12/0

Lea, a tough as teak full-back, was capped twice in the 1964-65 season whilst at Ipswich in games against Northern Ireland and Italy. Lea was made club captain after joining the club from Leyton Orient in 1964. He won the 1968 Second Division championship and had a brief spell as Town's caretaker manager before being appointed Bobby Robson's first-team coach in 1969. Lea later managed Colchester United for three seasons and scouted for George Burley at Portman Road.

CAPTAIN FANTASTIC: MATT HOLLAND BECAME A TOWN LEGEND DURING HIS SIX-YEAR SUFFOLK SPELL

WE'VE GOT AN IRISH INTERNATIONAL...

Alan Lee

Position ....Striker
Born ....Galway, August 21st 1978
Town Hello .... (H) Sheffield United, 14/1/06, FLC, D 1-1
Town Farewell .... (H) Wolves, 23/8/08, FLC, L 0-2
Town/Intl Appearances 109/2
Town/Intl Goals... 34/0

The powerful Lee had already gained eight caps for the Republic before signing from Cardiff City for £100,000 in January 2006. A genial character who supplied a physical presence up front for the Blues, Lee had an excellent first season at the club. In a particularly magnificent performance at Southampton, he scored two superb goals in a victory at the St. Mary's Stadium. He left for Crystal Palace for £600,000 in 2008 but failed to settle before being relegated with Norwich City, whilst on loan, later that season.

PORTMAN ROAD LEGENDS

Jason De Vos

Position .... Defender
Born .... Ontario, January 2nd, 1974
Town Hello ....(H) Gillingham, 7/8/04, FLC, W 2-1
Town Farewell................................. (H) Hull City, 4/5/08, FLC, W 1-0
Town/Intl Appearances 179/6
Town/Intl Goals... 11/1

A strapping central defender, De Vos was signed by Joe Royle on a free transfer from Wigan Athletic in the summer of 2004. He was made captain after Jim Magilton left the club as a player and asserted himself with some excellent displays in a rather porous defence. De Vos represented Canada 43 times – scoring on three occasions – prior to joining Town and whilst at Portman Road he won six more caps for his country which included a goal and a booking in a World Cup qualifier against Honduras.

THE MEN WHO MANAGED THE TOWN

Joe Royle
Spell: October 2002 to May 2006
Honours: None
Overall Record: P 189: W 81 D 48 L 60 F 308 A 265

Jovial Scouser Joe Royle began his footballing career at Everton making in excess of 270 appearances for the club, scoring 119 goals. He hit 23 goals in their 1969-70 championship-winning season and won six caps for England. Following playing spells at Manchester City, Bristol City and Norwich City, he took over as manager of Oldham Athletic in July 1982, losing in the Littlewoods Cup Final to Nottingham Forest in 1990 before guiding the Latics to the Premiership in 1991. Oldham also reached two FA Cup semi-finals during Royle's twelve years at the club. He joined his beloved Everton where he won the FA Cup in 1994 before a spell at Manchester City from where he was sacked after relegation to Division One in 2001. Royle joined Town after the dismissal of George Burley and narrowly missed out on a play-off spot that season, but guided the team to successive play-off semi-finals in 2003/2004 and 2004/2005 (losing on both occasions to West Ham United). He left the club by mutual consent in May 2006 following a 15th place finish in the Coca-Cola Championship in 2005-06 – Town's worst league finish in over 40 years. He currently is manager of his first club Oldham Athletic.

STOKES IS NO JOKE

Bobby Stokes' shock late winner for Southampton over Manchester United in the 1976 FA Cup final meant Town were denied a place in Europe despite finishing sixth in Division One. Despite it being their lowest finish in four seasons, Town had beaten Manchester United 3-0 only weeks earlier at Portman Road but it was the Red Devils who claimed the final place in the Uefa Cup following the defeat.

JOINING THE RANKS

Welshman Oswald Parry was signed as Ipswich Town's first ever professional player in June 1936. The tough-tackling full-back joined from Crystal Palace and made 104 league appearances for the Blues before retiring in 1949.

THE MEN WHO MANAGED THE TOWN

Jim Magilton
Spell: June 2006 to April 2009
Honours: None
Overall Record: P 147: W 56 D 40 L 51 F 203 A 182

Magilton, a former Liverpool apprentice, enjoyed a playing career at Oxford United, Southampton and Sheffield Wednesday before a loan move to Town in January 1999 which was made permanent just over a month later. Captain of the side during the 2003/2004 and 2004/2005 campaigns, 'Magic' made 315 appearances for the Blues. Highly regarded by the Portman Road faithful, Magilton, who was capped 52 times by his native Northern Ireland, will long be remembered for the hat-trick he scored in the play-off semi-final defeat of Bolton Wanderers in May 2000 that earned Town a place at Wembley and, ultimately, promotion to the Premiership. Following the departure of Joe Royle at the end of the 2005/2006 campaign, Magilton became his surprise successor despite no previous managerial experience. After three years in the job, he was sacked on April 22nd 2009, the day after Simon Clegg was appointed as the club's new chief executive, after failing to turn Marcus Evans' investment into tangible success on the pitch.

McCRORY SEES RED

In April 1950, Belfast-born inside-forward Sam McCrory became the first Ipswich player to be sent off since Town joined the Football League in a 5-0 drubbing at Aldershot. He was dismissed alongside Aldershot's John Cropley for fighting, with fifteen minutes to go. McCrory was an interesting character. He joined Town with Linfield colleague Jim Feeney for a record £10,500 transfer fee in the 1949/50 season but he was slow to settle in East Anglia and left to join Plymouth Argyle before forging a fine career at Southend United. He scored on his debut – and only cap – for Northern Ireland in a 3-2 win against England at Wembley in November 1957. At the age of 33 he was the oldest post-war player to make his debut for his country.

SUPER FAB

Born August 23rd 1970 in Suriname, Fabian Wilnis was a gifted Dutch defender who enjoyed a marvellous career at Portman Road after signing from De Graafschap in January 1999. He joined as a replacement for Mauricio Taricco, and despite playing as a full-back in Holland, Wilnis had to quickly adapt to a wing-back role under manager George Burley's system. It was great credit to Wilnis that he settled in so well following his debut in a 1-0 reverse at home to Grimsby Town on January 9th 1999 in Division One. He gave away the free kick that led to the goal on that day and was substituted for Titus Bramble on a nervy debut but he began to impress the coaching staff and scored his first goal in a 6-0 thumping of Swindon Town at the County Ground only three months later. After missing out on a Wembley appearance in the 2000 play-off final despite starting 33 games that season, he made an instant impact on his first appearance in the Premiership when he scored with a sublime finish past Fabien Barthez in a 1-1 draw with Manchester United at Portman Road the day before his 30th birthday. A memorable season for Wilnis also saw him score the winner at Coventry City in November 2000 and he started 27 top flight games that season as Town finished a brilliant fifth. The next season, Wilnis found himself behind Chris Makin and Hermann Hreidarsson for the full-back positions and he struggled to establish himself in a team which surprisingly found itself relegated after such a successful first season back in the top tier. Following the appointment of Joe Royle as manager, Wilnis found himself back in favour in Division One and became a hero of the Town followers when he scored the opening goal in a 2-0 televised victory over Norwich City at Carrow Road in March 2003. He continued to offer fine service to the club and his consistency saw him win the supporters' Player of the Year title in 2005-2006 as he continued to defy his advancing years, earning himself a new contract in the progress. Despite being sent off twice against Plymouth Argyle during his Suffolk career, Wilnis finally clocked up 325 appearances at Town and scored six goals in his nine years and, after failing to win a place on the coaching staff, joined Grays Athletic in August 2008 before enjoying a well deserved Town testimonial against Colchester United in July 2009.

THE MEN WHO MANAGED THE TOWN

Roy Keane
Spell : April 2009 to January 2011
Honours : None
Overall Record : P 81 W 28 D 25 L 28 F 63 A 94

New owner Marcus Evans sent a signal of his intent to return to English football's top flight when appointing Roy Keane as Town manager only two days after sacking Jim Magilton. Keane, a former Manchester United legend who won seven Premier League titles, had resigned as manager of Sunderland only five months earlier after leading them to the Championship title in his debut managerial season in 2006/2007. He had steered the Mackems to Premier League safety in his first season at football's top table but resigned due to irreparable differences with the club's owners and investors.

BRILLIANT TOWN SCOOP TITLE

Town clinched their first honour as a professional club with the Division Three (South) title in April 1954. The title was clinched with a 2-1 victory at Newport County before a crowd of 11,258 who witnessed goals by local legend Tom Garneys and Scottish forward Willie Callaghan to cap promotion for the Blues. A solid and consistent outfit all season, Ipswich were seven points clear at the turn of the year and were defeated only twice in their first 32 games of the season. It was due reward for manager Scott Duncan, after years of patient rebuilding at the club, which also saw eight consecutive league wins posted as well as Tom Garneys finishing top scorer at the club for the third straight season.

FANTASTIC FENN CLINCHES LEAGUE

Town registered their first ever league championship title with a 2-1 win at runners-up Eastbourne FC in 1922. Arthur Fenn's brace saw Town win the Southern Amateur League and ensured 4,000 fans welcomed the Blues back to Ipswich Station that night. Fenn was a nippy striker who scored 57 goals in 94 starts for the club.

CHOPPING UP THE OPPOSITION

Derek 'Chopper' Jefferson was born in Northumberland on September 5th, 1948 and made 175 appearances for the club between 1967 and 1972. He joined as a trainee, before making his senior debut on January 28th 1967 in a 4-1 FA Cup win over Shrewsbury Town, as a replacement for Bill Baxter. Although this was his only appearance in the 1966-67 season, he broke into the first team in the following campaign and was a regular as the club won the Second Division championship in fine style. Jefferson gave the club excellent service over the next few seasons; he made more first-team appearances than anyone else in the 1968-1969 season. In that season, he scored his only Town goal when he pounced to net at Tottenham Hotspur in a 2-2 draw. During his spell in Suffolk he became the first player to be sent off at Portman Road and only the second in a Football League match when he was dismissed for a wild lunge on Alan Birchenall as Chelsea visited Portman Road on Boxing Day, 1968. Dave Webb, a future manager of the Pensioners and Southend United, scored a hat-trick that day as Chelsea won 3-1. Jefferson admitted himself that it was a wild lunge with the ball a full ten yards away from where the incident took place. Town gaffer Bill McGarry had recently left the club to join Wolverhampton Wanderers and Cyril Lea was managing the side that day – it would not be long before Bobby Robson arrived at Portman Road. Jefferson was a rugged, intimidating central defender who flourished under the abrasive McGarry at Portman Road and he linked up again with his old boss in October 1972 when he moved to Molineux. Despite joining Wolves, he never became a first choice player, managing 52 appearances in total for the club over four years, before he was loaned to the North American Soccer League in the summer of 1976 – playing for the Boston Minutemen and the Washington Diplomats – before joining Sheffield Wednesday during October 1976. The following month, he left Molineux for good and joined Hereford United, playing in the second tier for the only time in their history. After finishing his playing career, Jefferson became reserve team manager at Birmingham City under Jim Smith before leaving after five years at this post to devote himself to Christian work – which he is still involved with – acting as a sports coach in a church-affiliated programme in Solihull.

STEIN TO THE RESCUE

On a dramatic final day to the 1993-94 season pint-size Mark Stein's injury-time winner for Chelsea against Sheffield United at Stamford Bridge meant the Blades were relegated instead of the Blues. Town drew 0-0 at Ewood Park and claimed the point which was enough to keep them up thanks to Stein's late clincher in a 3-2 win. Ironically, the South African-born striker was signed on loan by George Burley four years later and scored against Charlton Athletic and West Bromwich Albion in an eight-game spell.

PENSIONERS SENT PACKING

In May 1920, Town, then still an amateur side, defeated First Division and FA Cup finalists Chelsea 1-0 in front of a record crowd of 8,000 at Portman Road. Len Mitzen's fine shot on 55 minutes gave Town a famous win in a charity match made possible by Suffolk-based Earl Cadogan's friendship with the London side.

IPSWICH v IPSWICH

Brilliant defender and club skipper Mick Mills won the bragging rights over fellow Blues defender Allan Hunter as England thumped Northern Ireland 4-0 at Wembley in May 1976. Also playing that day were future manager Joe Royle, as an England substitute, and Northern Ireland's Bryan Hamilton, who had recently left Portman Road to join Everton after 199 appearances.

JOHNSON THE MASTER

England's 2-2 Home Championship draw with Wales in May 1975 at Wembley featured two Town players. David Johnson scored both goals on his England debut while Colin Viljoen gained his second and final cap. Three days later Johnson scored again, alongside Kevin Beattie, in a 5-1 thumping of Scotland. Johnson was a powerful Liverpool-born forward who joined from Everton in November 1972 and went on to score 46 goals for the club in four seasons. He left to join home-town club Liverpool in a dream £200,000 move and was seen supporting Ipswich in the 1978 FA Cup victory over Arsenal at Wembley despite hobbling on crutches and with a leg in plaster.

THE MEN WHO MANAGED THE TOWN

Paul Jewell
Spell : January 2011 to October 2012
Honours : None
Overall Record : P 86 W 30 D 18 L 38 F 122 A 147

Scouser Jewell replaced Roy Keane in October 2012 after notable success managing Wigan Athletic and Bradford City. His first match ended in a 2-1 defeat to Millwall and during his spell he enjoyed highs but mainly lows. West Ham were thrashed 5-1 at Portman Road and Barnsley were beaten 5-3 live on Sky Sports when Town were 2-0 down and on the back of seven consecutive defeats. The news of his departure was tweeted by young French midfielder Cheick Kourouma "Le coach est parti".

WE'VE GOT A WELSH INTERNATIONAL...

Gavin Williams

Position .... Midfielder
Born .... Merthyr Tydfil, July 20th 1980
Town Hello .... (A) Coventry City, 19/11/05, FLC, D 1-1
Town Farewell .... (A) Colchester United, 5/4/08, FLC, L 0-2
Town/Intl Appearances 59/1
Town/Intl Goals 3/0

Attacking midfielder Gavin Williams represented Wales against Cyprus just six days after joining Town in November 2005 on loan from West Ham United and three days before a goalscoring debut for the club at Coventry City. After a promising yet injury-ravaged spell in Suffolk he finally joined Bristol City for £100,000 in June 2008 so he could be nearer his family in Wales. A signing that, on paper, looked a good one, his career at Portman Road never took off.

ANIMAL MAGIC

At the end of the 1921-22 season whippet racing was seen for the first time at Portman Road as the club tried to generate extra income. Whippet sprint racing started as a professional sport after World War I, with its height in the 1920s and 1930s, but died out not long after as a result of the beginning of World War II. At the same time, new groundsman Walter Wollard kept chickens, goats and sheep under the Portman Road stand.

ON YER BIKE

Four days after finishing 17th in Division One, Town went down 2-1 to an East Berlin XI in an end-of-season friendly watched by 70,000 fans in May 1963. The Blues scored early through a Ted Phillips header but the hosts fought back to win with two late goals. The game finished five minutes early so as not to clash with the end of the Prague-Warsaw-Berlin cycle race. The race, known as the 'Peace Race' was first held in 1948 and was known as the 'Tour de France' of the East.

JOINING THE BIG BOYS

Monday May 30th 1938 was another momentous day in Ipswich Town history. At a meeting in London, it was announced that Town, with 36 votes, would be elected to the Football League for the following season. Exactly 60 years after Ipswich Association were formed, Ipswich Town would make their debut in professional league football and an amazing journey was to begin.

NELSON'S BLOOMERS

After a magnificent 1980-81 season Ipswich lost 2-1 to NASL side Calgary Boomers, owned by Canadian businessman Nelson Skalbania. He became famous for signing 17-year-old future ice hockey legend Wayne Gretzky to the World Hockey Association. Skalbania had earlier purchased an ice hockey team called the Edmonton Oilers in 1975. With debts of $1.6m during 1976, he took on Peter Pocklington as a partner. Pocklington gave Skalbania a vintage Rolls Royce Phantom, used in the film *The Great Gatsby*, and a diamond ring worth about $150,000 in a deal worth about $700,000, according to Pocklington, who also agreed to take on half of Oilers debt.

DYER THE FLYER

A tremendously gifted youngster, Kieron Dyer – born in Ipswich on December 29th 1978 – came through the fabled youth ranks at Portman Road as a dazzlingly skilful midfield starlet. He first appeared on the scene as a substitute for Mick Stockwell days before his eighteenth birthday as Crystal Palace were despatched 3-1 on Boxing Day 1996. His full debut came a week after at a snowy Nottingham Forest who crushed Town 3-0 in the FA Cup third round under the temporary management of Stuart Pearce. It was in 1997-98 when Dyer really blossomed, earning plaudits around the division for his consistency and his skill, scoring a lovely goal in a 2-2 draw at Huddersfield Town and becoming increasingly influential as Town reached the play-offs, but lost to Charlton Athletic. He ended the season being selected for the PFA First Division select-team and earning two England 'B' caps after 52 starts for the club. His star continued to rise in the 1998-99 season as some amazing displays saw him both called into the full England squad and play for the PFA First Division side again. In March 1999 he scored in a 3-2 win over Watford in Division One, despite fracturing his leg earlier in the game, and after returning from the injury his two goals in a 4-3 thrilling win over Bolton Wanderers in the play-offs were not enough to gain Town's place in the final. It was obvious that his talent was becoming too burgeoning for the second rung of English football and that summer he became the first English signing by Newcastle United manager Ruud Gullit who signed him for £6.5 million. He burst onto the scene in the 1999-2000 season, scoring his first Toon goal against Sunderland in a 2-1 defeat which saw Gullit resign shortly afterwards. Additionally, he finally earned an England call-up when he appeared in a 6-0 victory over Luxembourg under Kevin Keegan where he featured at right-back. However, injuries began to bite at St. James' Park and although he made three appearances from the bench in the 2002 World Cup finals for England, Dyer was in and out of the Newcastle team before making the 2002-03 PFA Premiership team of the season and captaining the club. He joined West Ham United for £7 million in 2007, after 251 appearances, where he broke his leg in one of his first Hammers outings and many now wonder if this talented player will add to his current total of 30 England caps.

WE'VE GOT A JAMAICAN INTERNATIONAL...

David Johnson

Position ....Striker
Born .... Jamaica, August 15th 1976
Town Hello ...... (A) Wolverhampton Wanderers, 15/11/97, D1, D 1-1
Town Farewell................(H) Tottenham Hotspur, 20/12/00, PL, W 3-0
Town/Intl Appearances 158/4
Town/Intl Goals... 62/2

David Johnson, a livewire forward who was impressively influential during his time in Suffolk, had an interesting international career. Having played, and scored, for Jamaica against the USA at the beginning of September 1999, and having appeared for the England 'B' side, he accepted an invitation to join the Welsh squad. Only injury prevented him from pulling on the red shirt but by the time the next international squads were announced he had pledged his future to Scotland, only to discover that he was ineligible.

WE'VE GOT A WELSH INTERNATIONAL...

Geraint Williams

Position ....Midfielder
Born .... Treorchy, January 5th 1962
Town Hello ....(H) Aston Villa, 18/8/92, PL, D 1-1
Town Farewell....................................(A) Stoke City, 7/2/98, D1, D 1-1
Town/Intl Appearances 264/2
Town/Intl Goals... 3/0

Pint-sized midfielder Geraint 'George' Williams gained two caps at Ipswich to add to the eleven he acquired as a Derby County player. These two appearances came a few years apart; in the 1992-93 season he played against the Republic of Ireland and in the 1995-96 season against Germany as a substitute. The tigerish battler made his debut in Town's inaugural performance in the Premier League in 1992 and gave solid service before joining Colchester United on a free transfer whom he later managed.

THE FATE OF FEENEY

Jim Feeney, a stylish left-footed defender, was born in Belfast in June 1921. Joining from Swansea City, Feeney was a virtual ever-present for six seasons after making his debut in 1950 and went on to win two caps for his country. In his 232nd and final appearance against Brighton & Hove Albion he broke his nose after six minutes and had to leave the pitch – Town went on to lose 3-0.

HOW'S THAT!

Future Town striker Mick Lambert was 12th man for England in the Lord's Test against the West Indies in June 1969. Lambert provided sterling service as a back-up striker at Portman Road during the 1970s and scored 45 goals before joining Peterborough United. He was a talented cricketer who was on the Lord's ground staff when he starred in the field that summer as England, chasing 332 to win, ran out of time with Geoff Boycott undefeated on 106.

NELSON THE LEADER

Cockney Andy Nelson, the popular captain of Town's 1961-62 league championship-winning side, was born in Silvertown on July 5th 1935. Nelson made 214 appearances without scoring a goal. He later managed Gillingham and Charlton Athletic before emigrating to Spain. Born close to Upton Park, Nelson was signed by Alf Ramsey from West Ham United for £8,500, a new club record, in May 1959. He captained the club in all league and cup games during the 1961/62 league championship season and was once ordered to do extra training after being caught hitching a lift on a sugar beet lorry when out on a six-mile road walk.

TOWN OVER THE MOON

On Sunday 20th July 1969, Town crushed Vancouver Spartans 5-1 with goals from Ron Wigg (2), Peter Morris, Charlie Woods and Frank Brogan. The crowd of 3,000 was considered locally to be disappointing, the counter-attraction of the first ever moon landing on TV being the explanation! On the day that the human race accomplished its single greatest technological achievement, Town recorded a fine win at the start of their pre-season tour.

JAMIE AND HIS MAGIC TOUCH

Initially called up to deputise for the injured Ian Marshall at home to Wolves in October 1995, James Scowcroft – born in Bury St. Edmunds in November 1975 – initially made use of his excellent aerial prowess and impressed supporters. He won a consistent place in the Town side in the 1996-97 season when he plundered 11 goals including doubles at Sheffield United and Bolton Wanderers, and also another against the Blades in the play-off semi-finals. His strikes at Bolton, who were leaders at the time, ensured a first home defeat of the season as Town pipped them 2-1 with Scowcroft grabbing an 88th-minute winner. His undoubted skill was recognised by regular England under-21 call ups, alongside Keiron Dyer and Richard Wright, but in the 1997-98 season he suffered a bad injury at Norwich City which kept him out for two months. He was carried off in a neck brace after being paralysed down one side and, after recovering, he then tore his cartilage in training. On his return he struggled to find his form, was sent off against Middlesbrough in a 1-1 draw and then found the David Johnson/Alex Mathie strike partnership kept him out of the side although England 'B' invited him into the squad for the game against Chile. In 1998-99, Scowcroft developed as a target man but suffered a torrid collarbone injury in an accidental collision with Barnsley goalkeeper Tony Bullock in December, weeks after scoring his first Town hat-trick in a 3-0 pasting of Crewe Alexandra at Gresty Road. It was the 1999-2000 campaign that saw him really flourish as he welded consistency with skill and, after playing in midfield and attack, was voted the club's Player of the Year with 15 goals despite missing out on an appearance at Wembley against Barnsley in the play-off final. When Town returned to the top flight of English football, Scowcroft started 22 games and scored four goals including the winner in a 2-1 victory at Leeds United early in the season. However, after scoring 55 goals in 256 games, Leicester City came calling in July 2001 and he arrived at Filbert Street for £3 million. Despite initially struggling due to injury he found his feet under Micky Adams and had scored 28 goals in 140 Foxes starts before joining Coventry City in July 2005 and then Crystal Palace in July 2006. Just before the move, he returned on loan to Portman Road as a replacement for the injured Shefki Kuqi but failed to hit the net.

THE MEN WHO MANAGED THE TOWN

Cyril Lea
Spell: November 1968 to January 1969
Honours: None
Overall Record: P 7: W 3 D 0 L 4 F 13 A 11

Cyril Lea was a former Town wing-half who, between 1964 and 1968, made 123 appearances for the club, was made club captain and also appeared twice for Wales. He was appointed caretaker manager for the period between Bill McGarry's departure and the arrival of Bobby Robson, just under two months later. After becoming a first team coach under Robson he left to join Stoke City after the FA Cup win in 1978 and later coached Wales before becoming boss at Colchester United for three years.

BADGE OF HONOUR

Following an *Evening Star* competition to find the best badge design, Town won 2-1 at Old Trafford wearing the Suffolk Punch horse on their shirts for the first time. Bryan Hamilton and Trevor Whymark scored in front of 51,459 fans. The shirts did not sport a crest until the mid-1960s, when they adopted a design featuring a gold lion rampant guardian on a red background on the left half and three gold ramparts on a blue background on the right half. The competition was won by the treasurer of the Supporters' Club, John Gammage. Each element of the new design was intended to represent the region. Gammage said at the time: "I regard the Suffolk Punch as a noble animal, well suited to dominate our design and represent the club. To complete the badge I thought of the town of Ipswich which contains many historical buildings, including the Wolsey Gate, and is close to the sea with a large dock area."

BUILDING FOR THE FUTURE

In August 1971, the new Portman Road stand was unveiled before a 0-0 draw with Everton. Costing £180,000 it provided nearly 3,500 seats, raising capacity to nearly 37,000, and was opened by Sir Alf Ramsey. Later that season Portman Road hosted an under-23 international between England and Switzerland when perimeter advertising arrived for the first time.

WE'VE GOT A WELSH INTERNATIONAL...

Lewis Price

Position	Goalkeeper
Born	Dorset, July 19th 1984
Town Hello	(A) Gillingham, 17/4/04, D1, W 2-1
Town Farewell	(A) Sheffield Wednesday, 9/4/07, FLC, L 0-2
Town/Intl Appearances	75/3
Town/Intl Goals	0/0

Although Price was born in Bournemouth, he qualified to play for Wales through a Welsh-born grandmother and had an eventual debut against Cyprus in November 2005 when he conceded a 42nd-minute penalty in Limassol. Price left for Derby County for £200,000 in July 2007 after 75 appearances and has seen subsequent loan spells at Milton Keynes Dons and Luton Town.

PORTMAN ROAD LEGENDS

John Elsworthy

Position	Wing-half
Born	Newport, July 26th 1931
Town Hello	(H) Notts County, 27/12/49, D3(S), L 0-4
Town Farewell	(H) Bolton Wanderers, 19/9/64, D2, L 1-4
Appearances	434
Goals	52

Many saw John Elsworthy as the greatest Welsh player never to be capped by his country. Rugby was his first love and he was spotted by chance by ex-Manchester United player Billy Owen while scouting for Town. An elegant player with an eye for goal, Elsworthy was listed in the Wales 22 for the 1958 World Cup Finals in Sweden but the Welsh FA reduced their travelling party to 18 players due to a lack of funds and he missed out. Along with Larry Carberry, Roy Bailey, Ted Phillips and Jimmy Leadbetter, Elsworthy became one of a small group to be the first and only players to win First, Second and Third Division championship medals with the same club.

FIRST-EVER FOOTBALL LEAGUE GAME

Saturday August 27th 1938

Ipswich Town	4-2 (2-0)	Southend United
Bryn Davies		*Thomas Bushby (2)*
Fred Jones (2)		
Gilbert Alsop		Att: 19,242

1. Mick Burns	1. George Mackenzie
2. Billy Dale	2. John Milne
3. Ossie Parry	3. William Forster
4. George Perrett	4. William Leighton
5. Tom Fillingham	5. John Trainor
6. Jimmy McLuckie	6. W. Carr
7. Jackie Williams	7. Len Bolan
8. Bryn Davies	8. Thomas Bushby
9. Fred Jones	9. Tudor Martin
10. Gilbert Alsop	10. Samuel Bell
11. Jackie Little	11. Robert Oswald

Town's Football League baptism arrived with a 4-2 Portman Road victory over Southend United, who travelled to the game by boat. The 19,242 fans in attendance witnessed a scintillating performance which drew the following plaudit from the *East Anglian Daily Times*: "It's early yet, of course, to make rash predictions but watch out for Ipswich Town! Here is a side capable of first-class scientific football, and although this is the club's first season in the league organisation, their players have an experience of wealth and talent. On this form, Ipswich Town should have a very successful season in their new sphere." The club finally finished a respectable seventh in Division Three (South).

LONDON MOURNING

Before the kick-off of Town's FA Cup thumping 5-0 reverse at Spurs on January 30th 1965 there was a minute's silence dedicated to Sir Winston Churchill who had been buried at a state funeral at St Paul's Cathedral only three days earlier. Jimmy Greaves scored a hat-trick for the Londoners with his Scottish strike partner Alan Gilzean grabbing the other two goals.

WE'VE GOT AN IRISH INTERNATIONAL...

Kevin O'Callaghan

Position .... Midfielder
Born .... Dagenham, October 19th 1961
Town Hello .... (A) Everton, 9/2/80, D1, W 4-0
Town Farewell .... (H) Everton, 29/12/84, D1, L 0-2
Town/Intl Appearances 148/17
Town/Intl Goals 5/0

During his time at Ipswich, diminutive midfielder O'Callaghan won 17 caps for his country and appeared in both their record defeat (7-0 in Brazil in 1982) and record win (8-0 against Malta in 1983). He was signed for £200,000 from Millwall in 1980 and was a useful squad player in Town's impressive spell at the top of English football in the early 1980s. He also featured in the football film *Escape to Victory* with Sylvester Stallone and Pele where his character in the story volunteered to have his arm broken so Stallone ('Hatch') could be freed from isolation.

WE'VE GOT A MACEDONIAN INTERNATIONAL...

Velice Sumulikoski

Position .... Midfielder
Born .... Struga, April 24th 1981
Town Hello .... (A) Sheffield Wednesday, 2/2/08, FLC, W 2-1
Town Farewell .... Current Player
Town/Intl Appearances 42/10
Town/Intl Goals 1/0

Signed for £500,000 from Bursaspor by Jim Magilton in January 2008 during the winter transfer window, the Macedonian midfield general has been on the periphery of the Town first team since joining, although he has shown glimpses of his potential and offers a physical presence in the middle of the park. He has won ten caps for his country whilst at Portman Road and has been a regular for Macedonia whilst trying to win a place in the Town line-up.

FROM SALTBURN TO WEMBLEY VIA IPSWICH

Tony 'Mogga' Mowbray was born in Saltburn on November 22nd 1963, and after supporting his local club Middlesbrough as a boy, he signed for the Teessiders in November 1981. He quickly proved himself to be a magnificent leader as the linchpin of a Middlesbrough team threatened by serious financial pressures and liquidation in 1986. He led the club, under the guidance of Bruce Rioch, to the Second Division title in 1987-88 and at the end of the following season he was called up, alongside defensive partner, Gary Pallister, for an England 'B' Tour. Mowbray also led his team-mates out in the Zenith Data Systems Cup final at Wembley in 1990 in a 1-0 defeat to Chelsea. However, Boro's spell in the top flight of English football lasted one season and, after selling Pallister to Manchester United for £2.3 million, Mowbray stayed a little longer before joining Celtic in November 1991 for £1million. He had scored 30 goals in over 400 appearances at Ayresome Park but unfortunately the injuries began to bite at Parkhead as he made only 96 appearances in four years before being signed for £500,000 by George Burley in October 1995. His debut was a 2-1 defeat at home to Wolves in October where he was immediately installed as captain. His early days at Portman Road saw him play with six different defensive partners in as many games. Just as he was finding his feet, Mowbray suffered a groin injury in February 1996 which kept him out of action for some time and it was not until the 1998-99 season that everything clicked into place as Town reached the play-off semi-finals and Mogga started in 46 games and helped the club to equal the club record of 26 clean sheets in a season. Although aging in years, Mowbray continued to be a commanding figure in the defence and kept his place as a player despite also being a first-team coach. His crowning glory was when he scored with a towering header to settle Town nerves in the 2000 play-off final where he captained the side to success. It proved the last of his 158 appearances for the Town and it was a fitting end to a marvellous Portman Road career. With Town back in the Premiership he turned to coaching and found himself caretaker manager before the appointment of Joe Royle in 2003. He later won managerial plaudits at Hibernian and West Bromwich Albion by playing an attractive brand of flowing football.

TOWN IN FREEFALL

Before Ipswich Town's first home match of the season against Coventry City on August 18th 1970, four free-fall parachutists from the Red Devils delivered the match ball to the Portman Road centre spot after jumping from 7,000 feet. Unfortunately, it had no impact as the Sky Blues won 2-0.

TUNBRIDGE TONKED

Town celebrated their first ever match as a professional team with a 4-1 Southern League thumping over Tunbridge Wells Rangers on August 29th 1936. In front of 14,211 spectators – which smashed the previous ground record – goals from George Dobson, Jackie Williams, Bobby Bruce and Jack Blackwell saw the Blues triumph. Queues had started to form by one o'clock in blistering sunshine and a band from the Queen's Scots Guards entertained the massed ranks. The club finished champions at the end of their first season as a professional club.

TOP-FLIGHT TRIUMPH

After winning promotion to the First Division the previous season, Ipswich began their journey in the top flight slowly with a draw and two defeats. When Burnley arrived in Suffolk on a Wednesday night in 1961, they were hot favourites after beating Town 4-3 a week earlier. However, the boys in Blue sent out a reminder to the division that they were a force to be reckoned with as they ran rampant and ran out 6-2 victors. Goals from Roy Stephenson, Doug Moran, Jimmy Leadbetter, Ted Phillips and Ray Crawford (2) saw the start of an amazing season under Alf Ramsey which led to the club becoming English champions at the very first attempt. Burnley were to finish eventual runners-up.

WAR DECLARED

On Saturday 2nd September 1939, Ipswich drew 1-1 with Norwich City in a Third Division (South) fixture. It was their last game for six years as Britain declared war on Germany the very next day, as Prime Minister Neville Chamberlain addressed the nation. Fred Chadwick, who scored Town's goal that day, was held as a prisoner of war by the Japanese a few years later.

THE AMERICAN BAKER

Gerard Baker, born on April 11th 1938 in New York City, was born to an English father and Scottish mother when his parents were temporarily living in the United States. When just a year old, his parents moved to Liverpool after his father decided to return to England on the outbreak of World War II. His father died in the hostilities and his mother and siblings moved to Scotland. He signed with Larkhall Thistle when he was 14 and played in six games before moving to Coventry City in June 1955. Baker spent one and a half seasons with the Sky Blues without getting a first team appearance. In December 1956, he moved back north to sign with Motherwell where he played thirteen games and scored four goals. In November 1958, he joined St. Mirren where he finally hit his stride as a forward. In April 1959, he scored the third goal in the Paisley side's 3-1 dismantling of Aberdeen in the Scottish Cup final, which was his eighth goal of the 1958-1959 competition. On January 30th, 1960, he scored ten goals in a 15-0 win over Glasgow University and by this time, top English clubs were beginning to notice. In November 1960, Manchester City paid £30,000 for Baker but he spent only a brief time at Maine Road before moving to Hibernian in November 1961 where he grabbed 43 goals in 84 games for Hibs before moving to Town in December 1963 for £17,000 – a then record signing for the club. He more than returned the investment by scoring 66 goals in 151 games and after a blank debut he scored in each of his next five appearances before netting league hat-tricks against Tottenham Hotspur and Blackpool. His hat-trick at White Hart Lane represented the only occasion in which a Blues player has scored three goals and finished on the losing side. He ended the 1963-64 campaign as top scorer and also led the club charts in the next two seasons before becoming unsettled, joining the transfer list and moving back to Coventry City in November 1967, where he scored five goals. Baker had dual US and English citizenship, and when it became apparent that he would not be selected for England, he made himself available for the US side. Baker joined the States as they began qualifying matches for the 1970 World Cup and his first cap came in a 4-2 defeat to Canada in October, 1968.

WE'VE GOT A NIGERIAN INTERNATIONAL...

Finidi George

Position ....Striker
Born .... Nigeria, April 15th 1971
Town Hello ....(A) Sunderland, 18/8/01, PL, L 0-1
Town Farewell .... (A) Slovan Liberec, 14/11/02, UC, L 0-1
Town/Intl Appearances 46/7
Town/Intl Goals... 8/0

George was signed for £3,000,000 from Real Mallorca in 2001 to a great fanfare and was expected to consolidate Town's position in the higher echelons of English football. However, a disappointing injury-plagued spell saw him last just over twelve months before moving back to the Spaniards on a free transfer. George won seven caps for the Super Eagles at Portman Road mainly in the 2002 African Nations Cup.

WE'VE GOT AN IRISH INTERNATIONAL...

Alex Bruce

Position ....Defender
Born .... Norwich, September 28th 1984
Town Hello ....(H) Crystal Palace, 5/8/06, FLC, L 1-2
Town Farewell... Current Player
Town/Intl Appearances 111/2
Town/Intl Goals... 2/0

Son of former Manchester United captain Steve Bruce, Alex is a committed defender, and had made a handful of appearances for his father's Birmingham City side before signing for the club on a free transfer in the summer of 2006. His wholehearted displays have seen him become a Suffolk favourite and his two appearances for his country whilst at Portman Road have come in friendlies against Ecuador and Poland. The popular Bruce signed a new two-year deal at the club not long after the arrival of Roy Keane.

GUSTAV THE GREAT

Dutch speedster Gustav 'Gus' Uhlenbeek joined Town on a permanent basis from SV Tops just before the start of the 1995-96 season after impressing during a summer trial. He was born in Paramaribo in the former Dutch colony Suriname in August 1970, but grew up in Amsterdam and began his career with Ajax, but only played twice for the first team. He left the Dutch giants and played for Cambuur Leeuwarden before joining SV Tops. A lightning quick winger with a tasty shot, Uhlenbeek was undoubtedly a speculative signing by the manager George Burley but after being switched to right-back for an Anglo-Italian Cup game against Brescia in October 1995 it appeared as if he had played in the position for years. He settled into the team well, scoring three goals, including the winner in a 3-2 victory at Watford which sparked a mini pitch-invasion from the Town fans along the side of the pitch. At the start of the next season, 1996-97, Uhlenbeek suffered a rash of injuries and was not truly fit until halfway through the campaign before he had an extended run in the side before suffering a broken foot during the play-off semi-final against Sheffield United. He battled through each game, refusing to come off, which meant that his injury only became worse and he was forced to have surgery during the close season. However, he was back on form in the 1997-1998 season with some flying performances down the wing and it was a real shame when he joined Fulham on a Bosman transfer in the summer of 1998 after 113 games and 4 goals for the club. In his first season with the Cottagers he helped them win the Second Division championship under Kevin Keegan's stewardship in 1998 scoring his only goal for the club in a 2-0 win at Wrexham. Although starting only 30 games by the river, Uhlenbeek left a cult hero when he joined Sheffield United in August 2000. Immediately a regular for the Blades, Uhlenbeek went on loan to Walsall in March 2002, who actually beat his employers, 1-0, to secure their First Division status. He left Bramall Lane after 55 appearances and joined Bradford City where he again established himself in the 2002-03 season before spells at Chesterfield, Wycombe Wanderers, Mansfield Town and Halifax Town then saw him retire in May 2007 after delighting and frustrating fans in equal measure. He had played for nine English clubs in twelve years and amassed nearly 400 appearances.

TOWN'S FILMSTARS

Not many players can boast to have played alongside Pele and the late Bobby Moore; starred alongside Michael Caine, Max von Sydow and a young Sylvester Stallone; and escaped from the clutches of the Nazis. Former Town stars John Wark, Russell Osman, Kevin O'Callaghan, Robin Turner and Laurie Sivell can and it all happened in the 1981 John Huston movie, *Escape to Victory*. Wark and company – plus Mike Summerbee (England and Manchester City), Osvaldo Ardiles (Argentina and Spurs) and Kazimierz Deyna (Poland and Manchester City) – starred in the classic World War II tale of the Allies versus the Germans. Laurie Sivell and Robin Turner played for the Wermacht and Pele's overhead kick in the final scene took one take. "It was great experience" recalled Wark in a Liverpool programme interview. "Bobby Robson asked us if we wanted to do a film. No one seemed that keen, but three or four of us said yes not knowing how big it would be. Suddenly we're with Sylvester Stallone, Michael Caine and Pele. Brilliant. We honestly thought we were going over there just to do football scenes, but then they started handing out scripts and we realised we had to act as well."

THE PIES AND THE PIPER

On Wednesday 14th September 1977, a Swedish pipe band led Town supporters through the town to see the Blues beat Landskrona Bois 1-0 in the first leg of their Uefa Cup first round game. Trevor Whymark scored the only goal of the game and was to score four more in the 5-0 second thrashing back at Portman Road a fortnight later. It was the Blues' first ever European encounter against a Swedish team and they finally succumbed to Barcelona in the third round.

RODENT RAGE

In 1926, then dominant Barclays Bank beat Town 3-1 at Portman Road in the Southern Amateur League in front of 2,000 fans. Incredibly, the game was held up when a number of rats were noticed and chased away from the grandstand. Groundsman Walter Woolard, who kept his sheep and goats underneath the stand, admitted that his livestock were influential in causing the infestation.

THE START OF SOMETHING BIG

A group of gentlemen gathered at Ipswich Town Hall on a rainy October evening in 1878 to form a football club. After a lengthy debate, Ipswich Association Football Club was born. Who would have thought that exactly 100 years later the FA Cup would sit in the trophy room of their creation?

TRACTOR NOISE

On a cold October Tuesday night in 1997 at St Andrew's, dynamic midfielder Matt Holland's 34th minute goal at Birmingham City sparked the first airing of "1-0 to the Tractor Boys" as Town fans responded to earlier gloating from their Midlands hosts about a lack of noise. The game finished 1-1 after a late equaliser by veteran defender and future Birmingham boss Steve Bruce. Holland, in his first season at Ipswich after an £800,000 move from AFC Bournemouth, went on to have a magnificent career at Portman Road and scored 46 goals in 314 games, as well as representing the Republic of Ireland (and scoring) at the 2002 World Cup finals.

BEST IS BEST

Bobby Robson's testimonial for Town was against an England XI in November 1979. A crowd of 23,284 saw George Best turn out in an Ipswich shirt in a 2-2 draw. Only eight years earlier, Best was to have two significant games against the Blues. On Saturday 4th September 1971 at Old Trafford, George Best earned a corner, took it himself, and scored directly against his namesake David Best to earn United a 1-0 win. Three days later the teams faced each other again at Portman Road in a League Cup tie. Again Best stole the show including an extraordinary goal: he released Brian Kidd down the wing with a great pass, then met Kidd's cross with a diving header which was palmed onto the bar only for Best, lying on the ground, to poke the rebound home. A second goal from Best sealed a 3-1 win for United and Best also had another inswinging corner hit the post. The result prompted sections of the crowd to call for Bobby Robson's head, and for Town chairman Mr John Cobbold to subsequently apologise to Robson for their behaviour.

WE'VE GOT A NORTHERN IRISH INTERNATIONAL...

Chris Casement

Position	Defender
Born	Belfast, January 12th 1988
Town Hello	(A) Crystal Palace, 18/3/06, FLC, D 2-2
Town Farewell	Current Player
Town/Intl Appearances	14/1
Town/Intl Goals	0/0

Flame-haired defender Casement was a key member of the squad that lifted the FA Youth Cup in 2005 and is equally adept in the centre-back and full-back positions. Although yet to establish himself in the Portman Road set-up he has enjoyed promising loan spells at Millwall, Hamilton Academicals and Wycombe Wanderers and won his first full cap for his country in a 3-0 friendly reverse against Italy in Pisa in June 2009.

WE'VE GOT AN IRISH INTERNATIONAL...

Dermot Curtis

Position	Striker
Born	Dublin, August 26th 1932
Town Hello	(A) Fulham, 6/9/58, D2, L 2-3
Town Farewell	(H) Aston Villa, 21/5/63, D1, D 1-1
Town/Intl Appearances	42/9
Town/Intl Goals	17/3

Curtis was a tricky forward who was a prolific scorer at Shelbourne in the League of Ireland, and Bristol City, before signing for Ipswich in 1958. He scored on his Town debut at Fulham although his final Portman Road record of 17 goals was spread over nearly five years. He was the second player to win an international cap while on Town's books (Billy Reid being the first) and was capped a total of 17 times by the Republic – nine of them came while he was plying his trade in Suffolk.

MATHIE THE HAT-TRICK HERO

A product of the Parkhead youth team, Alex Mathie, born in Glasgow, was a livewire striker who only appeared rarely for Celtic in senior action before moving to Morton in search of regular football in 1991. Mathie became a prolific scorer for the 'Ton and was top goalscorer in each of his two seasons, netting 44 times in 88 games. The Cappielow club eventually cashed in on Mathie when Newcastle United came calling and prised him away to St. James' Park for £285,000 in 1993 but he struggled to establish himself in the first-team set-up and in February 1995 George Burley paid the Geordies £500,000 for his signature after he had scored four goals in 29 appearances – mainly from the bench. He proved to be a fantastic signing and settled into life immediately at Portman Road as he scored on his Premier League debut against Southampton in a 2-1 win. The next season, 1995-96, saw him form a brilliant partnership in attack with Ian Marshall as Town put defences to the sword. Mathie scored in each of Town's first four games, including a brace against Stoke City, and a hat-trick in a 3-0 win over eventual champions Sunderland at Portman Road. When Marshall left in August 1996 for Leicester City, Mathie struggled to cope initially as the goalscoring burden fell squarely on his shoulders but began to relish the responsibility and scored nine goals in 17 games, including doubles against Fulham, Oldham Athletic and Crystal Palace, before he suffered a shoulder injury against the Eagles in a 4-1 triumph. The nature of his injury meant a long spell on the sidelines due to complicated operations but he returned to action in some style on a famous day against Norwich City in February 1998. Mathie cemented a place in Suffolk folklore when he scored a first-half hat-trick against the Canaries as the Blues demolished their great rivals in a memorable 5-0 win. Mathie began to form a superb partnership with new signing David Johnson, but found himself part of George Burley's rotation policy as three strikers were juggled around; Johnson, Mathie and Scowcroft. When Mathie was a permanent fixture on the bench in October 1998 he joined Dundee United for £700,000 after scoring 47 goals in 108 competitive Town starts. A spell on loan at Preston North End in September 1999 saw him help the club to the Second Division championship with four goals and he retired in 2003 after a spell at York City.

ALEXANDER THE GREAT: MATHIE CELEBRATES A GOAL AGAINST CRYSTAL PALACE IN 1995

GOALS IN EIGHT CONSECUTIVE GAMES

Tom Garneys – 8 consecutive games

1 v. Bristol City ....4-2 (H)
Division Two *2/11/1957*
1 v. Cardiff City ....1-1 (A)
Division Two *9/11/1957*
1 v. Liverpool..3-1 (H)
Division Two *16/11/1957*
1 v. Middlesbrough ....2-5 (A)
Division Two *23/11/1957*
1 v. Leyton Orient ....5-3 (H)
Division Two *30/11/1957*
1 v. Charlton Athletic ....1-4 (A)
Division Two *7/12/1957*
1 v. Doncaster R...................................2-0 (H)
Division Two *14/12/1957*
1 v. Blackburn R...................................2-1 (H)
Division Two *21/12/1957*

Ted Phillips – 8 consecutive games

1 v. Bristol Rovers ....1-1 (A)
Division Two *3/9/1960*
1 v. Brighton..4-2 (A)
Division Two *7/9/1960*
1 v. Liverpool..1-0 (H)
Division Two *10/9/1960*
2 v. Brighton..4-0 (H)
Division Two *13/9/1960*
1 v. Rotherham Utd. ....1-1 (A)
Division Two *17/9/1960*
2 v. Southampton.................................3-3 (II)
Division Two *24/9/1960*
1 v. Leeds United ....5-2 (A)
Division Two *1/10/1960*
1 v. Charlton Ath. ....2-0 (A)
Division Two *8/10/1960*

FRANTIC FULHAM FARE

On Thursday December 26th 1963, Town suffered their joint worst defeat when Fulham pulverised them 10-1 at Craven Cottage. Graham Leggat scored a hat-trick in just three minutes – the fastest ever recorded in First Division history – as the Londoners raced to a 5-1 interval lead. Gerard Baker scored Town's goal while Bobby Robson scored for the hosts. Incredibly, just two days later, Ipswich gained sweet revenge with a 4-2 pasting of the Cottagers at Portman Road with a team showing just one change. Despite Leggat scoring again, Ipswich's goals were shared between Billy Baxter, Danny Hegan, Joe Broadfoot and Baker. Almost 35,000 fans witnessed the two games which provided 18 goals in 180 minutes.

THE BOYS IN BLUE

Ipswich Town's top 20 all-time appearances
(including as sub) since 1936 are:

Mick Mills	741
John Wark	678
Mick Stockwell	610
Paul Cooper	575
George Burley	500
Tommy Parker	475
Billy Baxter	459
John Elsworthy	434
Jason Dozzell	416
Doug Rees	386
Russell Osman	385
Frank Yallop	385
Eric Gates	384
Richard Naylor	374
Jimmy Leadbetter	373
Colin Viljoen	368
Allan Hunter	355
Ray Crawford	353
Terry Butcher	351
Roy Bailey	346

SAINTS ALIVE

In January 1961, Town suffered a record FA Cup trouncing as they surprisingly went down 7-1 at Southampton in the third round. Town went into the game at The Dell on the back of four wins having scored 16 goals in the process but they found themselves shell-shocked after going in at the interval 6-0 down. It was a mere blip in a momentous season, as Town were to go on to win the First Division title (and also draw twice with the Saints in the league that season).

GONE WITH THE WIND

In November 1911, a fierce gale saw the roof of the stand at Portman Road blow off. It was replaced for the princely sum of £60.

DOG DAYS

Town's game against Gillingham in November 1952 was relatively unmemorable as it finished 1-1. The crowd saw Willie O'Callaghan put Ipswich ahead before Ken Lambert equalised for the Kent side. Lambert's goal came about following an interruption when a dog ran onto the pitch near the end of the game. From the following drop-ball, the ball reached the striker who lashed home.

JOHNNY FOREIGNERS

In 1891, Town's first game against foreign opponents saw a surprising defeat to the Canadian/American Tourists 2-1 at Portman Road. Town paid the visitors £20 to play the fixture, the 35th match of a very long tour.

HAVENG A LAUGH

On December 6th 1924, Willie Havenga, Town's first overseas player, was born in Bloemfontein, South Africa. He set up two goals on his Town debut against Torquay United in 1952 and scored three goals in 19 league games. Havenga had a trial at Birmingham City a few seasons previously alongside his South African compatriots and joined Luton Town, before arriving at Portman Road.

WE'VE GOT A NORTHERN IRISH INTERNATIONAL...

Gareth Macauley

Position .... Defender
Born .... Larne, December 5th 1979
Town Hello .... (H) Preston North End, 9/8/08, FLC, L 1-2
Town Farewell .... Current Player
Town/Intl Appearances 39/6
Town/Intl Goals... 0/1

A towering and domineering central defender, Macauley was snapped up from Lincoln City by Jim Magilton for a sizeable fee of £1,500,000 in June 2008. After slowly settling, he turned in some excellent performances in his first season and was awarded the captain's armband. Macauley was capped ten times before joining Ipswich and has won a further six caps (to date) during his time at Portman Road – enjoying a goalscoring performance against San Marino in a 3-0 win in February 2009.

Kevin Wilson

Position .... Striker
Born .... Banbury, April 18th 1961
Town Hello .... (H) Gillingham, 26/1/85, FAC, W 3-2
Town Farewell .... (A) Charlton Ath., 17/5/87, D2 Play-Off, L 1-2
Town/Intl Appearances 123/3
Town/Intl Goals.. 49/0

A nippy striker with an excellent scoring record for the Blues, 'Jockey' Wilson joined Town from Derby County for £150,000 at the beginning of 1985. He scored on his debut against Gillingham and was a bargain buy when funds were low thanks to the poor decision to develop the Pioneer Stand without arranging previous funding. He joined Chelsea for £450,000 in June 1987 where he scored 42 goals in five years and won 42 caps for Northern Ireland. Going into the 2009/10 season, he is the manager of Ilkeston Town in the Blue Square North.

SEDGLEY SENT TO COVENTRY

Steve Sedgley was born in Enfield in May 1968 and grew up an avid Spurs fan. Although he often trained at White Hart Lane in his schoolboy days, and appeared in the youth team, the north London outfit did not offer him a contract and he joined Coventry City in 1986. He made his league debut against Arsenal in August and although he appeared in 25 games that season, he was too young and inexperienced to be included in the Sky Blues 1987 FA Cup final side which beat Spurs 3-2. After three years of solid progress at Highfield Road he found himself the subject of a dream move to Spurs who offered Coventry £750,000 for his services. Sedgley was signed to provide defensive stability and he went on to fulfil a dream denied to him four years earlier when he won a winner's medal against Nottingham Forest in the 1991 FA Cup. Spurs won 2-1 in a tremendous match at Wembley. He appeared in 222 league and cup games for the White Hart Lane outfit before Town made him their first £1 million player when he was signed in June 1994. At Portman Road, Sedgley proved to be a versatile performer who could feature in midfield or defence and in his first season he scored four goals as the club finished 22nd and were relegated from the Premier League. That season started slowly as a shin injury delayed his debut which came against Norwich City in a 2-1 home defeat in September 1994. As soon as George Burley was appointed manager, Sedgley was made captain just before finishing the season on the bench. In the following 1995-96 season the Londoner performed well, whether it was in central defence, midfield or even as a sweeper and his competitive and aggressive leadership saw him turn into a crucial player for the club. In addition, his tackling and ability at dead-ball situations meant he took virtually every corner, free kick and penalty. Despite suffering from a foot injury, Sedgley continued to play through the pain barrier clocking up 125 Blues appearances, with 18 goals, before joining Wolverhampton Wanderers in July 1997 in exchange for Mark Venus and £500,000. Whilst Venus turned out to be an excellent addition at Portman Road, Sedgley suffered with more injuries and required an operation to remove a small bone around the knee which limited his opportunities at Molineux. In December 2000, he had totalled 124 outings for Wolves and retired from league football.

SEDGE THE LEDGE: VERSATILE STEVE SEDGLEY AT PORTMAN ROAD IN 1994

SINGING THE BLUES

The full lyrics to Ipswich Ipswich (Get That Goal) as performed by the 1978 FA Cup final squad:

Der duh duh, Der duh duh, Der duh duh, Der duh duh duh,
Der duh duh, Der duh duh, Der duh duh, Der duh duh duh
We're all going to Wembley, that's where we belong,
So get on board we're going up, we're going to win the cup
Ipswich fans are cheering, to help us on our way,
We'll play the ball and win the game, It's going to be our day
Ipswich, Ipswich kick that ball, won't you get that goal for me,
Gimme, Gimme Ipswich Town, going to make some history, Ipswich
Ipswich, Ipswich get that goal, won't you win that cup for me, Ipswich,
Gimme, Gimme Ipswich Town, the best at Wember-ley, Ipswich
Der duh duh, Der duh duh, Der duh duh, Der duh duh duh,
Der duh duh, Der duh duh, Der duh duh, Der duh duh duh
We're going to be the champions, we'll gun those Gunners down,
And carry off the FA Cup, back to Ipswich Town
So come on everybody, and give your everything,
Clap your hands and stamp your feet, and everybody sing
Ipswich, Ipswich kick that ball, won't you get that goal for me,
Gimme, Gimme Ipswich Town, going to make some history, IPSWICH
Ipswich, Ipswich get that goal, won't you win that cup for me, IPSWICH,
Gimme, Gimme Ipswich Town, the best at Wember-ley, IPSWICH
Super-blues, Are just the best, super-blues, we'll beat the rest,
Ipswich, Ipswich kick that ball (get that goal), won't you get that goal for me,
Gimme, Gimme Ipswich Town (win that cup you see), IPSWICH
Ipswich, Ipswich kick that ball, won't you get that goal for me,
Gimme, Gimme Ipswich Town, going to make some history, IPSWICH
Ipswich, Ipswich get that goal, won't you win that cup for me, IPSWICH,
Gimme, Gimme Ipswich Town, the best at Wember-ley, IPSWICH

AWAY MISERY

Town have lost every away league match played at Carlisle United (four) and Wigan Athletic (two); and they have never won at Brentford, Cambridge United, Doncaster Rovers or Oxford United in the league.

THE MEN WHO MANAGED THE TOWN

Adam Scott Duncan
Spell: November 1937 to August 1955
Honours: Division Three (South) Champions 1953/1954
Overall Record: P 505: W 205 D 113 L 187 F 796 A 778

Adam Scott Duncan was born in Scotland and worked as a law clerk before winning the league championship with Newcastle United in 1908/1909 as a forward and managing Manchester United to the Second Division title in the 1935/1936 season. Duncan resigned from Old Trafford after they were relegated the following season and joined Town who were then in the Southern League. The chairman, Captain Cobbold, had personally driven to Manchester to appoint him after a tip from the secretary of The FA, Sir Stanley Rous. He stayed at Portman Road for 18 years, won one championship and remained as secretary for three years after being replaced by Alf Ramsey. A testimonial in his honour saw Town defeat Norwich City 3-1 at the end of the 1957/1958 season.

THE MEN WHO MANAGED THE TOWN

Jackie Milburn
Spell: May 1963 to September 1964
Honours: None
Overall Record: P 56: W 11 D 12 L 33 F 75 A 146

Milburn was a north-east legend who won three FA Cup winner's medals with Newcastle United during the 1950s and scored 200 goals in 395 games. He scored ten goals in thirteen games with England after World War II and after a spell managing Linfield he joined Southern League Yiewsley as player/manager. Appointed Town manager in 1963, he took over an aging squad and was relegated from the First Division in the 1963/1964 season after conceding 121 goals – including a 10-1 reverse at Fulham. After a poor start to the 1964/1965 season, he began to suffer from poor health and resigned, moving into the newspaper world and reporting on north-eastern football for almost 20 years before being inducted into the English Football Hall of Fame in recognition of his services to football.

OLE, OLE, OLE, OLE, PABLO, PABLO

Born in Redondela, Spain on August 9th 1979, Pablo González Couñago began a promising youth career with Celta Vigo in 1995, prior to making his professional debut on loan for Numancia in 1998. Although uncapped at full international level, Counago achieved a good under-21 record, scoring nine goals in 15 appearances, in addition to six goals in 13 caps at under-20 level. He was also joint top-scorer and received the Golden Shoe in the 1999 FIFA World Youth Championship, scoring twice in the final. In 2001, then Ipswich Town boss George Burley signed the out-of-contract striker on a four-year deal, following an impressive brace for the Spanish under-21s against England at St. Andrew's. Counago made his debut for the club in September of that year, coming on as a substitute for future boss Jim Magilton in a 1-0 away defeat to Sunderland. His first year was largely limited to cameo appearances from the substitute's bench, making just one start during Ipswich's Premier League campaign, which culminated in relegation to Division One. However, Counago did play for half an hour at the San Siro, coming on for Finidi George in the second leg of the 4-1 Uefa Cup defeat to Inter Milan. By his second season he'd established himself as a first-team regular, scoring 16 league goals in 28 starts, the first coming in the 85th minute of a 6-1 mauling of Leicester City; the second following five minutes later. Perhaps the highlight of Counago's Ipswich career to date came in that season, as he scored a memorable Uefa Cup hat-trick in the 8-1 demolition of Avenir Beggen of Luxembourg. In August 2005 Counago returned to his homeland, having amassed 31 goals in 99 appearances for the club. In July 2007, 50 appearances and 10 goals later, fresh from a two-year stint at Malaga CF, the prodigal son returned to Suffolk, scoring an hour into his Portman Road return against Sheffield Wednesday, securing a 2-1 victory for the home side. That year, his audacious back-heeled goal in a 3-1 defeat to Charlton Athletic was voted the best goal of the 2007/08 Championship season. Despite this, his season was marred by spitting allegations following a 2-1 win against Scunthorpe United. Counago and Scunthorpe's Jack Cork were both sent off, with the Scunthorpe players accusing the Ipswich striker of spitting at defender Andy Butler. Counago scored his 50th league goal for the club in the final game of the 2008/09 season at home to Coventry City in a 2-1 win.

WE'VE GOT A SLOVENIAN INTERNATIONAL...

Amir Karic

Position	Defender
Born	Slovenia, December 31st 1973
Town Hello	(H) Millwall, 26/9/00, LC, W 5-0
Town Farewell	(A) Birmingham City, 31/1/01, LC, L 1-4
Town/Intl Appearances	3/19
Town/Intl Goals	0/0

Feisty full-back Karic was signed for £700,000 from Slovenian champions NK Maribor in the summer of 2000 but never settled at Portman Road. Indeed, he didn't start once for the club while in Suffolk and his contract was terminated before he joined Crystal Palace. He played only 30 minutes of football before being substituted and never appearing for the Eagles again. Although never starting for Town, he won 19 caps for Slovenia in that spell which included a red card against Switzerland.

WE'VE GOT A WELSH INTERNATIONAL...

Billy Reed

Position	Winger
Born	Rhondda, January 25th 1928
Town Hello	(A) Walsall, 19/8/53, D3(S), W 2-0
Town Farewell	(A) Bristol Rovers, 1/2/58, D3(S), L 1-3
Town/Intl Appearances	169/2
Town/Intl Goals	46/0

Christened the Stanley Matthews of the Third Division due to his dribbling skills, Reed was capped twice by Wales whilst at Ipswich and has the distinction of being the first player to be capped whilst on the Town's books. His two appearances were in games against Scotland and Yugoslavia in the 1954-55 season. He helped the club win the Third Division (South) title in 1953-54 before heading back to Wales and playing for Swansea City.

MAURICIO THE MAGNIFICENT

Buenos Aires-born defender Mauricio Taricco was able to play at full-back or in midfield, with a preference for the right-hand flank. Due to having an Italian father, Taricco was able to play without a work permit under EEC rules when he joined Town in 1994. Able to also speak English, he arrived at Portman Road in September from Argentinos Juniors for £175,000 and made his debut in the home leg of the Coca-Cola Cup tie against Bolton Wanderers, who fielded two wingers and won 3-0 at Portman Road. Following that baptism of fire, in which he struggled to cope defensively, the young Argentine was next brought into the side the following season at left-back due to an injury to the consistent Neil Thompson. He seemed much more comfortable in the position and flourished in the number three spot, becoming more influential and combining brilliantly at times with winger Stuart Slater. The following season, 1996-97, saw Taricco in magnificent form which culminated in him being voted the supporters' Player of the Year. He grabbed his first goal for the club in a 5-2 drubbing of Reading, then claimed the only goal in a winning display at Stoke City before opening the scoring in a 2-0 victory over Norwich City later in the campaign. The following season saw Jamie Clapham arrive at Portman Road and, importantly, a switch to right-back which was crucial in producing a wonderful unbeaten run which took Town to the play-offs and eventual defeat to Charlton Athletic. However, Taricco's impressive contribution was recognised as he was named in the PFA Nationwide Division One select team and he continued to impress the Suffolk faithful at the beginning of the 1998-99 term before suffering an injury at home to Wolverhampton Wanderers in November. It was to be the last of his 170 appearances for the club, in which he scored seven times, before Town announced he was joining Tottenham Hotspur for £1.8 million – a tidy profit on the initial purchase! He settled in well at White Hart Lane and quickly became a consistent performer before needing a hernia operation. He returned, but suffered with uncharacteristic disciplinary problems before scoring his first Premiership goal in 2002-03 against Leeds United in a 2-1 win. After 156 appearances in six years at Spurs he was snapped up by West Ham United on a free transfer in 2004 but he left the Hammers after sadly suffering a career-ending injury on his debut against Millwall.

FIRST DIVISION PLAY-OFF FINAL 2000

Monday 29th May

Ipswich Town	4-2 (1-1)	Barnsley

Mowbray 28   *Wright (og) 6*
Naylor 52   *Hignett (pen) 78*
Stewart 58
Reuser 90   Att: 73,427

1. Richard Wright	20. Kevin Miller
25. Gary Croft	34. John Curtis (Nicky Eaden)
24. John McGreal	18. Chris Morgan
5. Tony Mowbray	31. Steve Chettle
6. Mark Venus	11. Darren Barnard
3. Jamie Clapham	8. Craig Hignett
8. Matt Holland	28. Keith Brown
11. Jim Magilton	7. Eric Tinkler (Geoff Thomas)
14. Jermaine Wright (Fabian Wilnis)	9. Matty Appleby
9. David Johnson (Richard Naylor)	10. Bruce Dyer (Georgi Hristov)
27. Marcus Stewart (Martijn Reuser)	11. Neil Shipperley

After three consecutive Division One play-off failures Town made it fourth time lucky at Wembley to earn a place in the Premiership, worth an estimated £10 million. After a nail-biting 5-3 play-off semi-final win over Bolton Wanderers at Portman Road, the Blues celebrated a fully deserved victory. The game was action-packed with six goals (one an own-goal), two penalties (one saved) and a gilt-edged chance for Georgi Hristov to make it 3-3, only for Richard Wright to save his header. On just six minutes Craig Hignett's fierce shot struck the crossbar and rebounded against Richard Wright's shoulder, who could do nothing as the ball crossed the line. Mowbray, Town's player-coach, who appeared in 39 games after 'retiring' the summer before, equalised with a textbook header in the 28th minute. Just before half-time Hignett pushed the ball past Wright, who caught the Barnsley midfielder, but then dived to his right to save Darren Barnard's penalty to send Ipswich into the break on level terms. Seven minutes after the restart they took the lead when Richard Naylor controlled Marcus Stewart's knock-down and, as Kevin Miller advanced, Naylor kept his nerve to score. In the 59th minute

Stewart made it 3-1 when he headed Jamie Clapham's cross from the left wide of Miller but in the 77th minute Barnsley were awarded another penalty and this time Hignett made no mistake from the spot. In stoppage time, with Barnsley committed to attack, Ipswich broke and Martijn Reuser ran 40 yards before crashing the ball past Miller. The Premiership was within touching distance and reality came a couple of minutes later.

BROWN'S BLISTERING DEBUT

Jackie Brown, also referred to as either Johnny Brown or John Brown, was a tricky winger who played football for both Ireland teams – the IFA XI and FAI XI. He was born in Belfast in 1914 and began serving an apprenticeship in the linen trade and playing football for his works team, William Ewart & Son FC, when he was spotted by Belfast Celtic during the early 1930s. In 1934, while playing for Celtic, he was selected to play for the Irish League XI and he subsequently scored in a 6–1 defeat against an English League XI. In December 1934, shortly after his 20th birthday, Brown signed for Wolverhampton Wanderers, making his debut on January 12th 1935 in a 4–0 win over Notts County. Within three months of signing for Wolves, he made his international debut for the IFA XI, against England in a 2–1 defeat in February 1935. He scored his only goal for the IFA XI on October 19th 1935 in a 3–1 defeat to England. Although his time at Molineux saw him become an international, he failed to hold down a regular place at club level and in October 1936 left to join fellow Midlanders Coventry City after just 31 appearances for Wolves (and 7 goals). He stayed at Coventry for just under two years, making 73 appearances, scoring 29 times. In September 1938 he joined Birmingham City and during the final season before the suspension of league football due to World War II – 1938-39 – he played 34 league games and scored 6 goals. As the war ended, Brown was playing for Barry Town before in May 1948, aged 33, he signed for the Blues. He made his debut for Town away to Bristol Rovers on August 21st 1948 in Division Three (South) and was outstanding in a crushing 6-1 victory. His next two games were 5-1 home wins against Torquay United and Newport County (when he scored his first goal for the club). However, only weeks later he featured in a 2-9 slaughtering at Notts County. Despite this, he finished with ten goals that season. He subsequently made 103 appearances and scored 27 goals for Town before retiring as a player in June 1951 when he made his last appearance for the club against Bristol City. He scored in a 2-0 victory.

GOALSCORING GREATS

The 1880-81 season witnessed the biggest win in Town's entire history when a 15-0 victory was achieved against East Stamford. John Knights registered three hat-tricks to become the highest ever individual scorer in one game. A mammoth 86 goals were scored in sixteen fixtures with the club still undefeated at home. The following season saw the club go undefeated with only Colchester Town (forerunner of Colchester United) able to hold the Blues to a draw. That season saw 16-year-old Stephen Notcutt make his debut. Notcutt served the club as player, captain and committee member for over forty years until his death in 1923.

WIGGING OUT

On January 5th 1968, the BBC *Match of the Day* cameras were at Portman Road for the first time and witnessed a 2-1 Division Two win over Birmingham City. The future champions earned the points thanks to a brace from newly signed striker Ron Wigg. The Essex striker's career started brightly with four goals in his debut season after signing from Leyton Orient in September 1967 and he notched a total of fourteen goals in his spell before joining Watford for a then record £18,000 in 1970. After leaving Vicarage Road after 20 goals in 90 starts, Wigg played for Rotherham United, Grimsby Town, Barnsley and Scunthorpe United before moving across the pond and working for the United States National Staff Coaching Board.

THE GREAT RIVALRY BEGINS

League football arrived at Portman Road in 1899 when Town finished a respectable fourth in the Norfolk & Suffolk League which featured the club's first ever league match with Norwich CEYMS which ended in a 1-1 draw. Two men of the cloth, the Revd M. W. Murray and Revd H. A. P. Gardiner, were frequent members of a side that won the Suffolk Senior Cup for the first time in four years with a 3-1 final win against Sudbury and retained the Ipswich Charity Cup for the fourth consecutive year. Complaints by the Ipswich & East Suffolk CC about damage to their crease resulted in the relocation of the football pitch at Portman Road to its present-day location – it was previously aligned from East to West on the area now covered by the practice pitch.

HOME SWEET HOME

Between 1878 and 1884, Town played at two grounds in Ipswich; Broom Hill and Brook's Hall, but in 1884, the club moved to Portman Road and have played there ever since. At their new home, Ipswich became one of the first clubs to implement the use of goal nets, in 1890, but the more substantial elements of ground development did not begin until, in 1901, a tobacco processing plant was built along the south edge of the ground. The first stand, a wooden structure, was built on the Portman Road side of the pitch in 1905. In 1911 the roof was blown off, and the ground was later commandeered by the British Army for the duration of the First World War. The club turned professional in 1936, and work began on the first bank of terracing at the north end of the pitch. The following year, on the back of winning the Southern League, a similar terrace was built at the southern 'Churchmans' end. All sides were terraced by 1954, and floodlights were erected in 1959 for use in lower light conditions. The two-tier Portman Stand was built along the east side of the ground in place of the existing terraces in 1971, and the west stand, then known as the 'Pioneer Stand' as a result of the club's sponsorship by the electronics company Pioneer Corporation, was converted to all-seating in 1990. In 1990, following the recommendations of the Taylor Report in the wake of the Hillsborough disaster the previous year, the terraces in both the north and south stands were also converted to all-seating, creating the first complete all-seater stadium in the top flight of English football with a spectator capacity of 22,600. Success on the pitch led to further investment in the infrastructure, with the club spending over £22 million on redeveloping both North and South stands, resulting in a current capacity of 30,311. In the past ten years, statues of both Sir Alf Ramsey and Sir Bobby Robson have been unveiled outside the stadium. The playing surface at Portman Road is highly regarded and has been voted best pitch in the league on a number of occasions while the current groundsman, Alan Ferguson, has received a number of accolades, including both Premiership and Championship Groundsman of the Year. Town's record home attendance is 38,010 for a sixth round FA Cup match against Leeds United on March 8th 1975. With the introduction of regulations enforcing all-seater stadiums, it is unlikely that this record will be beaten in the foreseeable future.

MANAGERIAL MAYHEM AT GOODISON PARK

Sir Bobby Robson's first game, on January 18th, 1969, saw his team travel to Everton to face their third-placed hosts in front of 41,725 fans. It was a game which featured at least four prominent managers of the future and finished in a pulsating 2-2 draw. Ray Crawford scored twice, one of the goals a controversial finish which the Toffees claimed he handled while Crawford said the ball came off his shoulder. Future Town boss Joe Royle played up front for Everton and had a shot cleared off the line before Howard Kendall, who brought significant success to Goodison Park in the 1980s, crossed for Jimmy Husband to make it 2-2. In the dying seconds, Alan Ball, the pint-size midfielder who played for England in the 1966 World Cup final – and managed Southampton, Portsmouth and Manchester City – clipped the upright with a penalty as the Blues claimed a point in a memorable first game for Robson.

PORTMAN ROAD LEGENDS

Paul Cooper

Position	Goalkeeper
Born	Brierley Hill, December 21st 1953
Town Hello	(A) Leeds United, 20/4/74, D1, L 2-3
Town Farewell	(A) Charlton Athletic, 17/5/87, D1, L 1-2
Appearances	575
Penalties Saved	19 out of 49

'Super' Paul Cooper was signed from Birmingham City in 1974 for £23,000 after a heroic FA Cup semi-final performance against the then mighty Leeds United in 1973; although he had to wait a few years before establishing himself as Portman Road's number one. Over twelve seasons he made 575 outings and won the Player of the Year award in 1980/1981 – no mean feat in a multi-talented, successful team. He picked up FA Cup and Uefa Cup medals and put his extraordinary record of saving spot-kicks down to studying opponents' techniques and previous penalty placement extensively. Cooper was unlucky not to win a cap for England, mainly due to the outstanding form of fellow goalkeepers Peter Shilton and Ray Clemence during an outstanding era of English shot-stoppers.

SUPER COOPER: GLOVESMAN PAUL COOPER WITH THE 1980/1981 PLAYER OF THE YEAR TROPHY

MONEY MONEY MONEY

As of June 2009, the highest transfer fee received for an Ipswich player is £6.5 million, from Newcastle United for Kieron Dyer in July 1999, while the most spent by the club on a player was £4.75 million for Matteo Sereni from Sampdoria in July 2001 following the club's successful qualification for the Uefa Cup.

DASHING DALIAN

Dalian Atkinson leapt to prominence at Town as a teenager, impressing many fans with his speed in the 1986-87 season. His time in Suffolk was memorable for a wonderful hat-trick against Middlesbrough in a 4-0 win when the Teessiders included Gary Pallister and Tony Mowbray in defence. Atkinson moved to Sheffield Wednesday for £450,000, after 22 goals in 56 starts in Suffolk, where he formed a fine front partnership with David Hirst and then joined Aston Villa where he enjoyed another impressive partnership, alongside Dean Saunders. Atkinson is most often remembered for his magnificent solo goal against Wimbledon which won a BBC *Match of the Day* Goal of the Season competition and is loved by Villa fans for his inspirational performance and crucial goal in the 1994 League Cup final win against Manchester United. The partnership was broken in 1995 when both players were sold to Turkish clubs; Saunders to Galatasaray and Atkinson to Fenerbahçe. Atkinson failed to settle in Turkey and had loan spells with FC Metz and Manchester City before spells in Saudi Arabia and South Korea.

SUPER STEWART

Marcus Stewart, a tricky Bristolian striker, was a favourite at Huddersfield Town before signing for Town in the final run in at the end of the 1999–2000 season. The Blues were promoted to the Premier League at the end of the season ahead of Huddersfield due in no small part to Stewart's goals, with two crucially coming in the 2-2 draw at Bolton Wanderers in the play-off semi-final away leg, and he then scored another in the play-off final itself. He continued his great form for the next season being the Premier League's second-top goalscorer (and the division's highest English goalscorer) during 2000–01 with 19 goals for the club. Stewart now plys his trade for Exeter City in League One.

BACK OF THE NET

Ray Crawford is Ipswich Town's leading marksman of all time.
The top 20 all-time leading goalscorers since 1936 are:

1. Ray Crawford.. 227
2. John Wark.. 179
3. Ted Phillips 179
4. Tom Garneys 143
5. Paul Mariner.. 135
6. Trevor Whymark 104
7. Eric Gates 96
8. Tommy Parker 92
9. Alan Brazil 80
10. Jason Dozzell 73
11. Frank Brogan 69
12. Gerard Baker 66
13. Chris Kiwomya.......................................64
14. David Johnson (1997-2000) 62
15. Pablo Counago*.....................................58
16. Bryan Hamilton......................................56
17. Simon Milton 56
18. Darren Bent...55
19. James Scowcroft.....................................55
20. Colin Viljoen 54

* current player

APATHETIC ALDERSHOT

When Town started off in professional football in 1936/1937 they entered the Southern League. When they won away at Aldershot Reserves 2-1 that season, with goals from George Perrett and Jack Blackwell, they went top of the league although the game was seen by a crowd of 975 which to date is the smallest crowd to witness an Ipswich league away game since turning professional. George Perrett was a half-back who later ran a pub in Croft Street, Ipswich while Blackwell scored eight goals in 20 games that season.

FROM SUFFOLK TO THE SWALLOWS

Jean-Michel (Mich) D'Avray was a gangling South African-born forward, recommended to the Blues by former Town and England midfielder Colin Viljoen. D'Avray, born on February 19th 1962, made his debut as a substitute for John Wark in a 2-1 Portman Road victory over Southampton in November 1979 before making his full debut against Coventry City a week later which ended in a 3-1 defeat. When Town finished runners-up to Aston Villa the very next season in the First Division, D'Avray scored his first Town goal against Leicester City (featuring a young Gary Lineker) when he replaced Eric Gates in November 1980. He finally received his British passport in April 1983. He then won two England under-21 caps, scoring on his debut in a 3-1 win against Italy at Maine Road in the semi-final first leg of the European Championships. D'Avray finally established himself as a first-team regular in the 1984-85 season with 30 league starts and six goals as Town struggled to seventeenth place in the top flight. Over the next few seasons, D'Avray struggled with injuries and was in and out of the team. He made his final Blues appearance in February 1990 in a 4-1 loss at Oldham Athletic, who were inspired by a brace from future bubble-haired Town marksman Ian Marshall. D'Avray's final tally was 48 goals in 254 appearances. After a fruitless spell on loan at Leicester City in 1987, the South African joined his next club, Dutch outfit NEC Nijmegen, where he made 28 appearances between 1990 and 1992. D'Avray started his managerial career in 1991 with the Moroka Swallows in Johannesburg where he remained for just one season before moving to Cape Town Spurs. He was awarded the South African Coach of the Year award in 1993 before leading the Spurs to a league and cup double in the 1993–94 season. From 1993 to 1997 he coached the South African under-23 team, leading them out in 1994 for their inaugural game against Ghana. He coached the squad for a total of 28 games, his final match coming in December 1997 against Uganda. In 1998 he moved to Australia to join A-League team Perth Glory as assistant manager before becoming manager in 2001. He led the team to the league title in 2003 and 2004 and succeeded Lawrie McKinna as National Soccer League (NSL) Coach of the Year, winning the accolade in the 2003–04 season, the final time the award was made.

WE'VE GOT A WELSH INTERNATIONAL...

Mick Hill

Position	Forward
Born	Hereford, December 13th 1947
Town Hello	(A) Arsenal, 25/10/69, D1, D 0-0
Town Farewell	(H) Leeds United, 4/11/72, D1, D 2-2
Town/Intl Appearances	77/2
Town/Intl Goals	20/0

Hereford-born Hill started his career with Bethesda Athletic and joined Sheffield United in September 1965. His first-team chances were limited, making just 37 appearances for the Yorkshire club in four years. He moved to Town for £33,000 in October 1969 and scored 20 goals in 77 appearances. He was a traditional target man for most of his career who earned the nickname 'Mick The Flick' for his propensity to move the ball quickly and with guile when he received it. His first-team career ended with a total of 33 goals in 159 games.

THE DAWN OF A NEW ERA

In 2007, Marcus Evans bought an 87.5 per cent share in Ipswich, purchasing Ipswich Town's £32 million debts with Aviva and Barclays Bank and making £12 million available in funds for new players. The deal was finalised following an Extraordinary General Meeting on December 17th 2007, and although Evans does not personally sit on the Ipswich board, he likes to keep a tight control over his interests and, according to one newspaper, it is understood that he wants to recoup his money within five years, by which time he hopes Ipswich will be an established Premier League club again. On April 23rd 2009, Roy Keane was appointed manager of Town. The 37-year-old signed a two-year contract following the sacking of Jim Magilton, following Keane's statement that he was prepared to move from his Cheshire home and manage again in the Championship. Keane had been out of work since December 2008 when he resigned as Sunderland manager, having been in charge of the Premier League club for 27 months.

MR CONSISTENCY

Steve McCall was a magnificent left-back for Ipswich although his versatility allowed him to play in a number of positions. He made his name at Town, where his greatest achievement was winning the Uefa Cup in the 1981 season playing an influential part in the club's victory. He joined Ipswich Town in 1978 as an apprentice, being scouted from the north-west where Town legend Kevin Beattie was also born, and went on to make 340 appearances for Town, scoring twelve goals. Although never a prolific scorer at Portman Road, McCall scored twice in the Uefa Cup first round thrashing of Skeid Oslo in his first season as the Blues won 7-0. McCall won a regular place in the team during the 1980-1981 season and England under-21 and England 'B' honours followed soon after. A model of consistency, McCall was one of four ever-presents in the 1981-82 season as Town finished runners-up to Liverpool in the First Division and appeared in a record 166 consecutive games in the early 1980s, a spell that was broken after he broke his foot in a 2-1 defeat against Sheffield Wednesday in April 1985. In June 1987, McCall joined Sheffield Wednesday for £300,000 but his time at Hillsborough, spent over four seasons, was ravaged by injury and he collected only 36 appearances. In the midst of his spell at The Owls, McCall achieved a childhood dream by being loaned to his home-town team Carlisle United in 1990 where he spent only a few months making six appearances without a goal. Towards the end of the 1991-92 season, Steve was sent down south, being sold to Plymouth Argyle for £25,000, where he would go on to become one of Argyle's greatest ever players, winning Player of the Season two years in a row in 1993 and 1994, only the second player in Argyle's history to achieve such a feet (the other being Paul Mariner, one of Steve's ex-team-mates). McCall made 275 appearances in a total of six years at the club before enjoying a short reign as caretaker manager at Plymouth, being replaced by Neil Warnock. In 2001, Steve hooked up with former team-mate and close friend George Burley as European scouting co-ordinator in Suffolk and has been a scout, reserve team manager and first team coach. McCall is currently Town's chief scout, enjoying life back at the club his career started with almost 30 years ago.

MR. MCCALL: STEVE MCCALL JOINED THE COACHING STAFF AFTER AN ILLUSTRIOUS PLAYING CAREER

PORTMAN ROAD LEGENDS

Jimmy Leadbetter

Position ....Winger/midfield
Born ....Edinburgh, July 15th 1928
Town Hello .... (H) Bournemouth, 8/10/55, D3(S), W 1-0
Town Farewell...............(A) Tottenham Hotspur, 20/1/65, FAC, L 0-5
Appearances 373
Goals...49

Educated a stone's throw away from Tynecastle – home of Edinburgh side Heart of Midlothian – Leadbetter played for Murrayfield Athletic before joining the Royal Artillery for two years' National Service. After spells at Chelsea and Brighton & Hove Albion, Alf Ramsey brought 'Sticks' to Suffolk where his exceptional vision and anticipation, despite a slight and non-athletic build, were vital to a team which carried all before them, winning first the Third Division (South), then the Second Division, and finally the 1962 league championship itself. After leaving Portman Road, Leadbetter played local non-league football before returning to his native Scotland working as a driver delivering newspapers.

WE'VE GOT AN ENGLISH INTERNATIONAL...

Brian Talbot

Position .... Midfielder
Born ....Ipswich, July 21st 1953
Town Hello .... (A) Burnley, 9/2/74, D1, W 1-0
Town Farewell .... (H) Chelsea, 30/12/78, D1, W 5-1
Town/Intl Appearances 227/5
Town/Intl Goals.. 31/0

A combative central midfielder who started as an apprentice at the club in 1968, Talbot turned professional in 1972. Talbot won six caps for England with all five of them while at Ipswich in 1977. He was in the FA Cup-winning side of 1978. The all-action Talbot joined Arsenal in 1979 for £450,000 and won the FA Cup for the Gunners in 1979 which saw him score. This meant that Talbot is the only player to play for different cup-winning teams in successive seasons.

THE YOUNG GUNS

Town's youth set-up is rightly lauded as one of the finest in the country and has, from its very beginnings, developed some of the finest young footballers this nation has seen. The current set-up, which was given full Academy status in 1998, has twenty full-time apprentices who play under-18 and reserve football and approximately 100 schoolboys who play under-16 level down to under-9. Town have won the prestigious FA Youth Cup on three occasions – 1973, 1975 and 2005. The list shows the winning runs to each competition:

1973
First round .... Southend United (H) .... W 2-0
Gates, Turner
Second round ...... Orient (A) .... W 2-0
Turner, Vale
Third round .... Coventry City (H) .... W 1-0
Vale
Fourth round .... Bolton Wanderers (A) .... D 1-1
Vale
Fourth round (R). Bolton Wanderers (H) .... W 1-0
Vale
Quarter-final .... Swindon Town (A) .... W 1-0
Gates
Semi-final (1/2) ... Chelsea (H) .... W 1-0
Gates
Semi-final (2/2) ... Chelsea (A) .... D 0-0
Final (1/2) .... Bristol City (H) .... W 3-0
Vale 2, Turner
Final (2/2) .... Bristol City (A) .... D 1-1
Peddelty

1975
First round .... Orient (H) .... W 1-0
Wark
Second round ...... Bristol City (H) .... W 1-0
Kenny
Third round .... Fulham (A) .... W 2-1
Osman, Roberts

Quarter-final .... Arsenal (H) ....W 1-0
Geddis
Semi-final (1/2)... Huddersfield Town (A)...................................W 1-0
Bertschin
Semi-final (2/2)... Huddersfield Town (H) ....W 3-0
Roberts, Bertschin, Geddis
Final (1/2)............ West Ham (A)..W 3-1
O'Neill, Bertschin, Geddis
Final (2/2)............ West Ham (H) ....W 2-0
O'Neill, Bertschin

2005
Third round .... Portsmouth (H) ....W 3-2
Krause, Clarke, Haynes
Fourth round .... Stoke City (A) ....aet W 2-1
Craig 2 (1p)
Fifth round .... Aston Villa (H)..aet W 3-1
Craig, Lordan, Clarke
Quarter-final .... Colchester United (A)......................................W 5-0
Knights 2, Collins, Craig, Clarke
Semi-final (1/2)... Tottenham Hotspur (H) ....W 2-0
Trotter, Clarke
Semi-final (2/2)... Tottenham Hotspur (A)...................................W 2-1
Trotter, Collins
Final (1/2)............ Southampton (A) ....D 2-2
Lordan 2
Final (2/2)............ Southampton (H)..aet W 1-0
Upson

STAYING AT HOME

Lowest five home league attendances at Portman Road since 1936

3,116 v Leyton Orient .... 1952-53...........Division Three (South)
3,562 v Mansfield Town .... 1938-39...........Division Three (South)
3,589 v Mansfield Town .... 1945-46...........Division Three (South)
4,015 v Torquay United .... 1951-52...........Division Three (South)
4,108 v Torquay United .... 1952-53...........Division Three (South)

CHAMPIONSHIP CLINCHER 1962

Saturday 28th April 1962

Ipswich Town	2-0 (0-0)	Aston Villa
Crawford 2		Att: 28,932

1. Roy Bailey	1. Sims
2. Larry Carberry	2. Lee
3. John Compton	3. Aitken
4. Billy Baxter	4. Crowe
5. Andy Nelson	5. Sleeuwenhoek
6. John Elsworthy	6. Deakin
7. Roy Stephenson	7. McEwan
8. Doug Moran	8. Baker
9. Ray Crawford	9. Thomson
10. Ted Phillips	10. Dougan
11. Jimmy Leadbetter	11. Ewing

Town, with a team made up of virtual unknowns who had been widely tipped to go straight back down at the end of the 1961-1962 season amazed the nation by winning the Football League championship at their very first attempt. They clinched the crown with a 2-0 win over Aston Villa at a packed Portman Road after closet rivals Burnley hit the self destruct button in the run-in and the Blues stole home to take the title. Despite a slow start, with just one point from the first three matches, a 6-2 victory over Burnley marked the beginnings of a steady climb up the table and top spot was claimed in March. Leading scorer that season was Ray Crawford with 34 league and cup goals, who managed a brace on a famous day in Suffolk while strike partner Ted Phillips came second with 31 league and cup goals.

I DON'T LIKE CRICKET, I LOVE IT

Town's first foray into Twenty20 cricket ended in an honourable 'draw' after 'bad light' prevented their match against Ipswich and East Suffolk, at Chantry Park, from reaching a conclusion on August 2nd 2007. The home side batted first and scored 147 all out before the Blues amassed 145 for 13 prior to the 'darkness' persuading the umpires to take the players off. Town's star performer was Alex Bruce, 4 for 24, and 20 runs off the bat.

LEGEND

John Wark's spell at Anfield giants Liverpool saw him become renowned for his drinking ability with team-mate Jan Molby describing him as having "hollow legs". One famous Christmas fancy dress party saw a party starting at lunchtime with a visit to portly Sammy Lee's wine bar and the evening ending at tough defender Tommy Smith's nightclub. On one occasion Wark attended the birthday party of John Aldridge's dad on a Sunday night. The Portman Road legend finished at 2.30 am and reported for training only five hours later feeling "fine and putting in a good shift". Aldridge had left his father's party two hours before Wark but ended up at training "not his chirpy self". Wark passed his driving test after promising his examiner Anfield tickets but promptly lost his licence for two years after being caught drink driving. Additionally, nutrition was not high on the list of player priorities back in the 1980s, with Wark stating; "We all liked chips and with no canteen we would often send out to the local chippy after training."

IN LOVE WITH ROMEO

In 1981, Romeo Zondervan, a cultured midfielder, was voted Holland's most promising young player whilst on the books of Den Haag. He then joined FC Twente, and despite strong interest from Town, who had just won the Uefa Cup against Dutch giants AZ Alkmaar, the highly gifted Zondervan joined West Bromwich Albion for £225,000 in March 1982. After 82 appearances at The Hawthorns, Bobby Ferguson snapped him up in 1984 for a bargain £70,000 to replace Anfield-bound John Wark. Zondervan enjoyed a rollercoaster spell at Town in an eight-year spell that included a relegation to Division Two in 1986 and the fans' Player of The Year gong in 1987. That season, Charlton Athletic narrowly pipped Town in the play-offs but Zondervan finally achieved deserved success when he became an instrumental cog in the Division Two-winning team in 1992. He finally left Portman Road after 325 appearances and 19 goals and was capped 6 times for Holland (although not while on the club's books). After hanging up his boots, Zondervan became an agent before enjoying some scouting work for the Blues across Europe and beyond. Not surprisingly, he is the only Portman Road player whose surname has begun with a 'Z'.

WARK THE WARRIOR: JOHN WARK DOMINATES THE ACTION IN 1989

TOWN GOALSCORING DEBUTANTS

Since the Second World War, the following players have all scored on their Ipswich Town debuts:

1. Jack Connor (2) .... Leyton Orient .... D3(S)...... Aug 1946
2. Albert Day (3) .... Norwich City .... D3(S)....... Sep 1946
3. Stan Parker (1)................. Port Vale.................... D3(S)...... Nov 1946
4. George Clarke (1)............. Northampton Town . D3(S)......May 1947
5. John Dempsey (2) .... Bristol Rovers .... D3(S)...... Aug 1948
6. Frances McGinn (1) .... Crystal Palace .... D3(S)....... Sep 1948
7. Joe O'Brien (1) .... Bournemouth .... D3(S)...... Aug 1949
8. Neil Myles (2)................. Crystal Palace .... D3(S).......Dec 1949
9. Ray Warne (1) .... Plymouth Argyle...... D3(S).......Dec 1950
10. Tom Garneys (1) .... Southend United ..... D3(S)...... Aug 1951
11. George McLuckie (1) .. Walsall....................... D3(S)...... Aug 1953
12. Ron Blackman (1) .... Reading..................... D3(S)....... Oct 1955
13. Brian Siddall (1) .... Barnsley.................... D2............ Sep 1957
14. Dermot Curtis (1) .... Fulham .... D2 .... Sep 1958
15. Ray Crawford (2) .... Swansea City .... D2 .... Oct 1958
16. Charlie Woods (1)........ Brentford................... LC2 ...... Sep 1966
17. Colin Viljoen (3) .... Portsmouth .... D2.......... Mar 1967
18. Ron Wigg (2) .... Carlisle United .... D2............ Sep 1967
19. John O'Rourke (2)......... Cardiff City............... D2............ Feb 1968
20. Rod Belfitt (1) .... Wolves...................... D1........... Nov 1971
21. Keith Bertschin (1)........ Arsenal .... D1............Apr 1976
22. Jason Dozzell (1) .... Coventry City .... D1 .... Feb 1984
23. Kevin Wilson (1)........... Gillingham .... FAC4........ Jan 1985
24. Sergei Baltacha (1) .... Stoke City................. D2 .... Jan 1989
25. Mark Stuart (2) .... Watford..................... D2............Apr 1990
26. Steve Whitton (1) .... West Brom................. D2............ Jan 1991
27. Ian Marshall (1)............. Oldham Athletic ...... PL........... Aug 1993
28. Paul Mason (1) .... Oldham Athletic ...... PL........... Aug 1993
29. Adam Tanner (1)........... Leicester City .... PL.............. Jan 1995
30. Alex Mathie (1) .... Southampton............ PL............ Feb 1995
31. David Johnson (1) .... Wolves...................... D1........... Nov 1997
32. Gary Croft (1) .... Manchester City....... D1 .... Sep 1999
33. Neil Midgley (1)............ West Brom .... D1 ....Dec 1999

34. Marcus Stewart (1) .... Barnsley...................... D1 .... Feb 2000
35. Martijn Reuser (1)......... Fulham .... D1 .... Mar 2000
36. Shefki Kuqi (1).............. Watford.................... D1 .... Sep 2003
37. Darren Currie (1) .... QPR.......................... FLC........ Nov 2004
38. David Unsworth (1)...... Sheffield United ...... FLC .... Feb 2005
39. Nicky Forster (1) .... Cardiff City............... FLC........ Aug 2005
40. Gavin Williams (1) .... Coventry City........... FLC........ Nov 2005
41. Ricardo Fuller (1) .... Leicester City .... FLC......... Feb 2006
42. Kevin Lisbie (1)............. Preston North End... FLC........ Aug 2008
43. Jon Stead (1) .... Reading..................... FLC .... Sep 2008
44. DJ Campbell (1)............ Cardiff City............... FLC......... Oct 2012
45. Noel Hunt (1)................ Charlton Athletic ..... FLC........ Nov 2014

SEASON OF GLOOM

The 1949-50 season saw Town achieve their lowest finish ever in the Football League when they ended the campaign 17th in Division Three (South). Three wins in the last four matches over Swindon Town, Torquay United and Port Vale saw the Blues avoid applying for re-election and only one team, Newport County, conceded more goals – 98 to Town's 86. In a 5-0 thrashing at Aldershot, Sam McCrory became the first Ipswich player to be sent off in a Football League game that would then see a gap of another 18 years before the next dismissal of a Town player. Leading scorer was Stan Parker, with 15 league and cup goals, in a dismal campaign for the club.

THE MEN WHO MANAGED THE TOWN

Mick McCarthy
Spell : November 2012 to date
Honours : None to date
Overall Record : P 134 W 55 D 37 L 42 F 135 A 130

No-nonsense Barnsley born Mick McCarthy replaced hapless Paul Jewell in November 2012 and has transformed the fortunes of the Town thanks to steady progress in the Championship. Finishes of 14th, 9th and 6th in 2014/2015 are testament to his hard work in both rebuilding team spirit in the dressing room and slowly improving results on the pitch. Could 2015/2016 be the season Town make it back to the top table?

ACKNOWLEDGEMENTS

I'd like to express my gratitude to all those at Pitch Publishing, most notably to Dan Tester for the opportunity and good advice. Thanks Danno. Significant appreciation must be made to the following works of reference I have used, namely, *The Men Who Made The Town: The Official History of Ipswich Town FC from 1878* (John Eastwood and Tony Moyes), *The Who's Who of Ipswich Town* (Dean Hayes), *Ipswich Town: Head to Head* (Peter Waring) and the brilliant www.tmwmtt.com (Ralph Morris – please visit and donate).

I would also like to personally thank Matt Holland for accepting to write the foreword and also Auntie Sue for the loan of the cottage, numerous tuna rolls and a wireless connection across a blisteringly hot Suffolk week in March 2009. I would also like to thank my Mum and Dad – who I now realise, since becoming a parent myself, would have been wondering what the hell I was getting up to travelling the breadth of the country on British Rail and praying I got back in one piece. Thanks for never once stopping me following the club I will always love.